Shakespeare's
Julius Caesar

A Production
Collection

Shakespeare's *Julius Caesar*

A Production Collection

Comments by eighteen
actors and directors
in seven different productions,
illustrated with
101 photographs

B. S. Field, Jr.

Nelson-Hall ⊞ Chicago

AAA8100

Library of Congress Cataloging in Publication Data

Main entry under title:

Shakespeare's Julius Caesar.

    Includes index.
    1. Shakespeare, William, 1564–1616. Julius Caesar.
2. Shakespeare, William, 1564–1616—Stage history—
1950–   3. Shakespeare, William, 1564–1616—Stage
history—United States. 4. Caesar, C. Julius, in
fiction, drama, poetry, etc. I. Field, Brad S.
PR2808.S45   792.9   79–25076
ISBN 0–88229–440–7

Manufactured in the United States of America

10 9 8 7 6 5 4 3 2 1

Contents

Acknowledgments

I owe a debt to many people for their help in completing this book. Obviously, I owe a large one to the actors and directors that I interviewed and to the photographers whose work makes up such a large part of this book's material. To those whose names appear later in this text, I wish to express my gratitude for their patience and their help. I am only sorry that some of them, like the photographer, Carolyn Mason-Jones, and the director, Richard Spear, passed away before they could see in the book the proof of their contributions.

I owe debts of gratitude to others: to Wayne State University, which awarded me a grant to visit as many Shakesepeare festivals as I could manage in the summer of 1973, the basic research that made this book possible; to those who put up with me and put me up during my travels, Carolyn and Dave Field, Sam and Dave Bell; for helping me to put my copy into shape to my typist, Patty Lynam.

I am also indebted to those friends who helped me with the grant, with the drudgery of transcribing hours of tapes, and with my morale: Carol and Ed Chielens, Marilyn and John Nathan, Nancy Pogel and Ed Recchia, Ruth and John Reed. Writers of acknowledgments often leave their spouses for last; Mary Lee helped me from beginning to end.

Preface

My students taught me how to make this book. I teach the literature of the drama at Wayne State University, and I always assign students to attend a play and write a review of it. Sometimes I bring to class production photographs or slides of plays we are studying. The students enjoy trying to guess what play the picture represents, what scene, what line the actors are probably reciting at the moment.

I noticed that the students who had not participated in such a classroom exercise with production pictures invariably wrote much worse reviews than those who had. They seemed to have strange misconceptions about the way play texts relate to the production on a stage. Some of these I learned to anticipate. Students would complain in their reviews: "How come the actors never said on stage the footnotes from the play?" or "Why did Shakespeare put all that important stuff in footnotes instead of in the dialogue?" Those are two classics, but even those two caught me by surprise the first time I met them.

Other more subtle confusions are sometimes expressed in reviews that condemn, for instance, the actors because they crowd the stage too much. In going over the paper with the student reviewer, I point out that after all, the text of the play requires that all those people be on stage, and I ask the student how the crowding, then, could be the actors' fault. "You mean," comes the incredulous question back, "I was supposed to say that Shakespeare was wrong for making it so crowded?" I try to suggest that the director was perhaps the clumsy one, placing the actors on the stage and blocking the scene so that it looked awkward. The student, not having thought about that, suddenly wants to go back and look at the play again. In many places that would not be possible; that production of the play would be gone forever.

But not at Wayne. One reason it took me so long to learn the lesson my students had to teach me was that at Wayne the students *can* go back and look again. The Hilberry Classic Theatre plays continuously during the academic year, so students can always see the play a second time. They can usher and see it again for nothing, if they feel the need to correct their first impressions. Even so, eventually I noticed the connection between the exercise with production pictures and the quality of the play reviews. The students who have used pictures to talk about a play they are reading, and about the problems in producing it, while they still find things to say that surprise me, make judgments based not on ignorance but on their tastes. They have taught themselves, with an efficiency that all my classroom talk about it never could achieve, the kinds of problems to which they ought to be addressing themselves, not only in writing an assigned review, but in writing of any kind.

The students have, therefore, taught me over the course of several years what they need to help them with their writing: pictures. Usually I can arrange to get production photographs or slides of one of the plays we are studying in class. Studying the pictures is often made more fruitful when I can invite some of the actors from the Hilberry company who are in the photographs to discuss in front of the class what they had been trying to do in the scenes pictured.

Students in other places are not so fortunate. They cannot always see the plays they are studying at all. Rarely can they go back to have a second look at a production if they feel like it. Nor can they talk much with the actors; indeed, they cannot even see many photographs of a production of the play. This book then, is calculated to correct that defect for at least one play that is commonly taught in high schools and colleges. A production collection will not do as much for student writing about a play as will a teacher who knows the material. But it can help both the students and their teachers reach the end to which, after all, the study of the drama—of literature in general—is only the means: better writing.

Introduction

This is a book of photographs of modern productions of Shakespeare's *Julius Caesar*. Each photograph is accompanied by comments from the actors in the photographs on their aims for the scene pictured. The photographs are arranged according to the order of the scenes in *Julius Caesar*. This book does not contain a text of play itself, and although some readers know Shakespeare so well that they can enjoy this book without even looking at the play, most of us find it more interesting to go through a text and these production photographs at the same time. Indeed, one of the uses of this book is to supplement the text of *Julius Caesar* in a classroom. Some suggestions for writing assignments appear at the end of the book.

These photographs come from seven different productions of *Julius Caesar,* all of them between 1968 and 1976, ranging from those at the college level to those by New York professional companies, from Maine to Oregon, from Los Angeles to Washington, D.C. Some of the actors interviewed had starring roles in one or even two of these productions, but a number of them had only small parts. Some of the productions were put on with all elaborate settings, costumes, and lighting available on a modern stage; some were mounted with only the slimmest of technical resources.

Some readers may remark that despite the different conditions under which these seven productions of *Julius Caesar* were done, they seem similar. But readers who have had some experience in play production will notice that there are differences, and striking ones. These productions all started, of course, with the same text, Shakespeare's *Julius Caesar*. But that text is not a simple one; it offers problems to directors and to actors, problems that get different solutions according to the different conditions of each production.

As readers of the actors' comments that follow will notice, one of the main influences that accounts for differences among productions is the stage on which the play is mounted and the auditorium that faces it. Some of the productions described here, like the one in Stratford, Connecticut, at the American Shakespeare Festival, or the one in Ashland, Oregon, at the Oregon Shakespearean Festival, played on huge stages to big auditoriums. Other houses like the one in Monmouth, Maine, at Cumston Hall, or the Old Globe Theatre in Los Angeles, are quite tiny.

Another influence is the budget, which determines the elaborateness of the costumes, the number of extras for crowd scenes, the amount left over for washing costumes and therefore the amount of "blood" possible in the assassination scene.

A third influence is the "concept," the idea or ideals that the company brings to the text of *Julius Caesar*. Why do *Julius Caesar* instead of some other play? Sometimes, of course, the play is done simply because it is time to do it, as in many university and festival productions, but sometimes the play is produced with an eye toward the way it reflects on contemporary events. Although actors and directors seldom openly speculate on such connections, some productions of *Julius Caesar* in the 1970's seemed to link themselves to the Watergate scandals in Washington.

The "concept" is often a reaction against earlier productions of the play. Actors and directors keep two famous versions of *Julius Caesar* in mind. One of these was the Orson Welles "modern dress" production of the play. Even though it was last on stage in the late thirties, it is still very much part of the actors' folklore of the play. Welles used his production to reflect on contemporary events at the time, putting actors into black military uniforms in order to make them look like the dictators then ruling Italy and Germany. The other famous production is the movie starring Marlon Brando as Mark Antony, James Mason as Brutus, and Louis Calhern as Caesar. Many actors took the trouble to see that picture; others took some trouble to make sure that they did not see it until after they had acted in the play.

The "concept" leads a company to its decisions about costumes, about the set, about the text, and about casting the parts. All the productions shown here used "period" costumes, but not all of them used "Roman" as the period. The Oregon Shakespearean Festival, for instance, has a policy of doing plays in the manner of a production in Shakespeare's day as nearly as possible. Since the evidence indicates that in Shakespeare's time *Julius Caesar* was staged in what was then "modern dress"—that is, not in Roman but in Renaissance costumes—the Oregon group performs in Renaissance English costumes. A similar idea was displayed in the production at the University of Kansas, combining Renaissance "everyday" garments with "costumes" of Roman togas hung on the shoulders. Other productions used some variation of the idea of a toga, depending on the budget, on the size of the stage and the auditorium, and, of course, on the look of the set in front of which the costumes would appear.

The set in some cases was formalized or only sketchy. At

Oregon and at the Old Globe in Los Angeles, the setting is the same for every play—a permanent replica of the background that was behind Shakespeare's original productions of this play in London about 1599. At the Arena Stage in Washington, D.C., the audience is on all four sides of the stage, so any setting is limited to a treatment of the stage floor, to levels and platforms, and to stairs at the corners and edges. At the Hilberry in Detroit, on the other hand, and in Monmouth, Maine, large abstract standing elements were used—the Hilberry's against a dark background, and those for the Monmouth production against a lighted "sky-cyclorama."

These choices were in turn influenced by the budget, by the action that the company expected to put in front of the set, and by the size and shape of the stage and auditorium. The stage and auditorium at the Hilberry are very shallow and very wide; the stage at Monmouth is tiny, narrow, and shallow. The "sky-cyclorama"—a blue wall or a large, tightly stretched canvas sheet, lighted from the sides—was selected at Monmouth to give the illusion of depth to the stage and avoid the feeling that the action was cramped. At the Hilberry the back of the stage was kept in darkness and the full width of it used to compensate for the lack of depth, a choice made in part because of the way the battle scenes were to be staged, and because, thanks to the cutting of *Julius Caesar* used in that production, the Hilberry version of the play began with a battle scene.

Shakespeare's plays are almost always cut to some extent and sometimes reorganized and rearranged on a modern stage —except at festivals devoted in principle, like the one in Oregon, to doing them uncut. *Julius Caesar* is no exception. The very first scene between the tribunes and the citizens is often cut, as is the scene between Portia and Artemidorus, Act II, scene iv. It is common to reassign speeches among the minor characters in the fourth and fifth acts according to the needs of the actors, the limits of the cast, and the desire of the company to make it seem that the same minor characters reappear instead of introducing new ones at the end of the play. Not all such cutting receives critical approval from members of the audience who know the play. But it continues to be done in modern productions just the same.

All these general conditions affect the actors, but sometimes appear only indirectly in their comments. More direct influences on each actor are the qualities of his own physique and voice, those of the actors opposite him on the stage, the way each scene has been "blocked" or organized by the director, and other realities of acting on stage, such as the "feeling" that the costume gives, or the heat, or the receptiveness of the audience. Most important, of course, is the role each actor has been given.

Casting is a director's responsibility, but once he has chosen someone to play a role, it becomes the actor's responsibility to find some way to make that character seem human. Characters in *Julius Caesar,* for instance, all seem divided men, containing two opposing impulses that some actors find difficult to justify within the same personality. Some speak in their comments of a "subtext," a collection of ideas that they have in mind about the character's hidden as well as overt motives for behaving the way he does. The "subtext" helps an actor give the illusion to himself, and therefore to an audience, that the character's contradictions are psychologically sound.

Some actors, in discussing the way they study a role, speak as if the creation of a role were all done inside themselves; others speak almost entirely in terms of a mechanical technique for achieving certain effects. One can never tell from the talk about acting how the acting actually looked, but when coupled with photographs of the scene in question, we can at least recover some idea of what the actors were trying to do.

It used to be considered witty among teachers and college professors to sneer at actors of Shakespeare for not knowing anything about Shakespeare, and among actors of Shakespeare to sneer at teachers for knowing nothing about what happens on a stage or why. Some of that gap of misunderstanding has been closing recently. Scholars who may complain that the comments by the actors in this book are sometimes excessively simple or take too little into account are also scholars enough to know what happens in a theatre and on a stage. They realize that an actor is not a free agent; he is acting in a production with a "concept," with a text that has been cut and for which costumes and sets have been designed. And he has been given a role to enact within that pattern before being consulted.

Yet the actor, more than any other person involved in an enterprise such as a production of Shakespeare, is the one who takes the most personal risks; it is his "interpretation" of the role that will be judged by the public. It is he alone who takes the chance of hearing the audience breathing—or holding its breath—or yawning—out in the darkness of the auditorium. The actors' comments, then, have added value because they come from veterans who have been into the dangerous place and felt what it was really like. These are the people who have been bringing us Shakespeare, the ones who are the most directly concerned with seeing that the plays live on a live stage.

The methods followed for getting the actors' comments presented are simple in this book. I visited the actors, showed them the photographs that I had earlier collected of them in the play, and asked them to talk about what they had been trying to do. Later I edited their comments to eliminate most of the talk that always comes up about what was usccessful and what was not. Most actors are the first to admit that since they can never see themselves, the way an audience sees them while they are acting, they are in no position to talk about how well they did. Thus much of the talk about what worked and what did not can become mere gossip. However, the talk about what was tried, about the actors' aims and the company's aims, reflect ideas about how Shakespeare works on a stage, how audiences react, that are still imperfectly understood by modern scholarship, ideas very much worth recording.

A study based as much as this one on photographs has some limitations. These pictures are not really of actual moments during a production. These were almost invariably taken during the final rehearsal period, sometimes before all the details of the production had been settled, at a "photo call." The actors were perhaps called together for a special session and asked to run through certain scenes for the photographer, who then stopped them whenever he saw something worth recording, and had them do it over again for his lens. Thus some of these shots show costumes and props that were not used after all in the production, as the actors' comments point out. Often the lighting for the "photo call" it much brighter than for the actual production. And sometimes the actors have to "pose," holding still for a shot. Some photographs look considerably more stilted and awkward than the actual production ever did.

Thus the photographs cannot tell much about how well the play was performed. But they are good evidence of the aims of the production, and when coupled, as they are here, with comments from the actors who were in the photographs, they serve to recover from the past some of the ideas and ideals that those productions illustrated.

Julius Caesar:
Act I

The Hilberry Classic Theatre at Wayne State University in Detroit produced Shakespeare's *Julius Caesar* as part of its 1968-69 season. The Hilberry Classic is the only graduate acting company in the world presenting plays in alternate repertory. The actors are all graduate students who have qualified as members of the company by audition, and they participate in productions of five to seven plays, alternating nightly, for the entire academic year. Most of the actors spend about two years at Wayne for an advanced degree in acting, directing, or theatre technical work before taking jobs in professional or university theatre programs. As it happened, two of them, Denny Lipscomb and Richard Greene, who were in the Hilberry production of *Julius Caesar* in 1968, are both professional actors now and were by coincidence both in the same production of another Shakespeare play in New York City when they were interviewed about the photographs of the Hilberry production.

Denny Lipscomb played the role of Octavius Caesar at the Hilberry. He was asked, like all the actors interviewed for this book, to describe the aims of the production and his aims for the role, how those were influenced by such factors as the stage or the kind of audience that attends the plays there.

Denny Lipscomb on Figure 1:
I don't think that the Hilberry stage limited a production there, but it required a certain kind of staging because it is, well, not really a thrust stage, but there's no proscenium

3

to frame the action, just this wide apron stage that comes out a little. Since I played Octavius, I had nothing to do in the first half of the play, so I also played a member of the mob in that first part. There I am, holding up a sheaf of grain. I was on and off as a member of the populace for most of the show. I shouted noises from the Coliseum off-stage, while Brutus and Cassius were talking, all that. We ran all over the place, holding up those sheaves of grain, though of course it was not as disorderly as it looked. Every step was choreographed and counted.

I liked that opening scene, though we did not, in this production, start with that. The really interesting part about this production was that we started with the battles of Act V and then did a flashback to this procession and ran the show in order from then on. That first procession seemed to work for our audiences.

Richard Greene, who, played Cassius at the Hilberry in 1968, also thought the scene worked well.

Richard Greene on Figure 1:
This scene emphasized the pomp and ceremoney, set up the offstage life, the races, the multitudes, and gave us a counterbalance for the Cassius/Brutus exchange. The audience could imagine an event with the scope of the Superbowl.

David Regal, who played Casca in that Hilberry production of 1968, is now a director in his own right not far from the Hilberry, at the University of Detroit. He comments on the cutting too.

David Regal on Figure 1:
Aiming at high school audiences, we began the play with the battle scenes from the last act, so that we didn't have to start off with a lot of exposition and lots of talk. We started off with the blood and thunder, and then as in a

Figure 1. Caesar's triumphant entrance on his way to the Coliseum, Act I, scene 2, Hilberry Classic Theatre, 1968. Lower left, in dark robe, holding a sheaf of wheat, is Denny Lipscomb, here a member of the populace but later in the play, Octavius Caesar. Center, in dark toga, standing and facing front with no sheaf of wheat, is Richard Greene as Cassius. In front of him, pointing out Caesar to the soothsayer, is David Regal as Casca. On the step, in white tunic, is Mark Antony (Earl D. A. Smith); to his left, with hand raised, is Caesar (Jeff Tambor); to Caesar's left, a step down, Calpurnia (Pat Ryan); on her left, Brutus (E. Lee Smith). (Photo, Wayne State University Photo Services.)

5

flashback we went from battle sounds to "Here come all the costumes," and Caesar made his triumphal entry.

The late Richard Spear was not only a professor at Wayne State University, but also one of the directors at the Hilberry Classic Theatre. It was he who directed the production of *Julius Caesar* in 1968. He began his comments by pointing out that he was among those who had had the play spoiled for them in high school by what they went through to study it. Then he describes one of the most radical variations among those discussed in this book, the way he "cut" the play, that is, rearranged the sequence of the action.

Richard Spear on Figure 1:
I am not terribly thrilled about ever doing *Julius Caesar* again. I wasn't so thrilled about having to do it originally. The play needed to be done; we needed it as part of our season; so I agreed to do it. And though I got excited about it while doing it, I have not been all that fond of *Julius Caesar,* not since I was in high school and had to study it there. So we did a pretty straightforward job; there were none of those ideas, "I have a concept for this that I want to carry through!" It was pretty straightforward—except for the cutting.

This cutting of *Julius Caesar* was done with the fact in mind that many of the Shakespeare productions here at the Hilberry are seen by a large number of high school audiences. Furthermore, I myself had never seen a *Julius Caesar* in which I had enjoyed any of that battle in the second half, all that fighting. Inevitably directors take the persons who seem weaker as actors and put them in those roles in the second half, because the roles in the first half have always seemed to demand the better actors.

In addition, the directors of our Hilberry program, Leonard Leone, had once said that he'd thought it would be a good idea to do *Julius Caesar* like a film, with flashbacks. Though everyone had laughed when Leonard said that, I sat down with that in mind to make a cutting of the play that started with those battle scenes. It was a generalized battle; no one could tell then what it was, only that it was a battle. We took bits and pieces of this person's death, and that person's death, and killed everybody off. Then the ghost of Caesar crossed the stage, the lights dimmed, and we heard "Caesar! Caesar! Caesar!" from offstage, and the lights came up on the entrance of Caesar on his way to the Coliseum in the beginning of the play.

We continued from there in sequence with very little cutting, through the tent scene and then right into that battle, repeated the battle scene we had started with, and went to the end of the play. What surprised me about that cutting was that I didn't get one letter; nobody complained! I was expecting all those teachers to tell me what a horrible thing I had done, but nothing like that happened.

The Arena Stage in Washington, D.C., supports a resident professional company of actors who produce plays, modern and classic, for runs of a month or more all year round. The audience sits on all four sides of the acting area. The stage makes some things easier than they would be on a regulation stage, but other things are harder, as Robert Prosky, who played the title role of Julius Caesar at the Arena in 1974, points out.

Robert Prosky on Figure 2:
Shakespeare works extremely well in the round, and especially in as large an arena as this one. Our stage is a sort of pit, with raked rows of seats above and around for the audience. We came on from behind the audience, up over one of the entrances, by a platform that had been built up quite high, and a huge staircase that came down

to one corner of the stage. Carrying me on in that litter from that height down to the level of the stage, through the audience, made a very effective kind of procession. The biggest problem for me was just not to fall off the litter. The trouble was that because of that height, we—the two guys who carried the litter and I—we had to get up there in a blackout, and then they had to lift the litter, and then get me down those steps; a problem, to say the least.

Caesar did do strange things. There are weaknesses. There are doubts. There's fear. There's evidence of great courage and also of great cowardice. He was a superstitious man. Men with such large views of themselves must be afraid of being cut off, somehow. But Caesar didn't consider himself strange. It's always a mistake for an actor to decide that his character is a villain or a phony or whatever. An actor has to find within the character the things that make him work the way he does. Caesar's life was full of large accomplishment, physical as well as mental. He never considered himself to be a phony. Others, Cassius, might well do so. The audience might come to that conclusion. But the actor of Caesar has to find the man's own reasons for what he does.

On this stage an actor can't play it close to the vest. It's a huge cube of space on the Arena Stage. By the same token, there must be less fakery. He must have a true moment and then make it larger. But if it's a fake moment to begin with, then when it is made large, it shows up in all its awful deformity.

Another Octavius Caesar, this time at the Arena, was acted by Gary Bayer, and he too talks about the effect of the stage on the way the play was "blocked," on the positions of the actors on that stage.

Figure 2. Caesar's entrance on his way to the Coliseum, Act I, scene 2, Arena Stage, Washington, D.C., 1974. On the litter is Robert Prosky as Caesar; in foreground, Stanley Anderson as Mark Antony. (Photo, Alton Miller.)

Gary Bayer on Figure 2:
The director used the openness of the arena for staging it, as you can see from this first big entrance scene. He did have trouble, given this much space, with the crowds. There never were enough of us. Octavius has all his scenes in the second half of the play, so in the first half I played one of the rabble of Rome on both sides of the photograph here. It was difficult to get, in this arena staging, that feeling of masses of people. Only if we pushed forward a small mass at the head of an entrance, and then straggled some down behind them—and we did that later in rehearsals after these photographs were taken—could we get that effect.

Cumston Hall contains a small-scale replica of a large European opera stage. Each summer an acting company operating there largely on a cooperative basis, using some amateurs and some young professionals working for minimum wages, produces a series of plays, for the most part Shakespeare's. The stage has the normal proportions found in most older theatres, with the audience all on one side of the stage facing the action that is framed like a picture by a proscenium arch, the opening in which the front curtain of the stage is usually hung. William Wright, now a New York professional actor, played Mark Antony in *Julius Caesar* with the company's production of the play in the summer of 1973. He first describes how acting in that theatre had to be adjusted, and then he comments on the costumes.

William Wright on Figure 3:
The house in Cumston Hall in Monmouth, Maine, has a very small proscenium stage, but we increased the stage size by building a circular apron. The acoustics there are very bright with brilliant sound and a lot of echoing, since the house is built of plaster and wood with no curtaining to

cushion the sound waves. The seats were all wooden and squeaked a lot; there were street noises coming through open windows—there was no air conditioning and it was hot that summer. There were a lot of programs used for fanning as well, but an actor can't do much about any of this noise and distraction, except to talk above it. The house is small enough so the actor doesn't need to shout. Nor does an actor need any great "operatic" gestures; they would look absurd in that small theatre. We all had to pull down, to reduce, our acting, to be aware of our arms and bodies. On the stage we'd be no more than two body-widths away from each other so to yell or gesticulate in the "grand manner" would have been silly. However, one had to remember the balcony (which was almost always sold out) and play to it.

I thought the costumes were terrific. They were hard to wear, being authentically styled togas, hot on those summer evenings, being 100 percent wool. One could never rush putting a toga on; one needed to have a dresser drape it carefully. And it was hard to stand always with one elbow out, carrying the weight. But the weight gave a senatorial stature, a feeling of impressiveness to the actor. I was not pleased by my first scene costume, my mock goatskin, my Lupercal "racing shorts," mainly because I thought myself a bit overweight.

John-Frederick Jones was in two of the productions of *Julius Caesar* described in this book, one of them in 1976 at the Old Globe Theatre in Los Angeles, a small-scale replica of an English Renaissance theatre, where he played Brutus, and the other in little Cumston Hall in the summer of 1973, where he played Caesar in the same production in which William Wright played Mark Antony. Jones speaks about the influences on his acting, not in terms of the acou-

Figure 3. "Beware the Ides of March." Caesar faces the soothsayer, Act I, scene 2, Cumston Hall, Monmouth, Maine, 1973. Front row, left to right, Cassius (John Tormey); Brutus (John Fields); William Wright as Mark Antony; John-Frederick Jones as Caesar; Cicero (William Meisle); Calpurnia (Davida Manning; and Portia (Lee McClelland). (Photo, Arthur Griffiths.)

12

stics of the hall, as Wright does, but in terms of the ideas within *Julius Caesar,* a very different approach. Jones also points out some of the ways in which the budget influences the production.

John-Frederick Jones on Figure 3:
Both directors, in Los Angeles and in Maine, felt that the play must go pretty fast, and they both made it drive. But in both productions, because of a lack of money, Caesar was not represented as rich enough, powerful enough. He's got to be not just a man, but the embodiment of the State, so that when they kill him, they still haven't killed him. I don't think a production can do enough to help out the actor of Caesar. He doesn't have a lot of scenes, and he is very important.

In Monmouth, where I played Caesar, I felt personally that I was too young, that I couldn't command the stage like a Caesar should. Remember the movie, with Brando? As Caesar they used Louis Calhern, an actor of the old school, and it lent that flavor of the gap between him and the rest. A production cannot do too much to help the actor in that role, put him up on platforms, have people make obeisance to him, slaves come in and fall on the floor, do something to show that he's really got a lot of power. It's hard for an actor to do it alone.

But he can help himself by taking his time. Many productions that I have seen have just "tapped" the opening scenes. They don't make the audience realize on what a hair's breadth the whole plot hangs. For instance, in this scene, it should be a question of suspense whether Caesar will talk to the soothsayer or not. One of the ways to do that is for Caesar to take his time with his lines, to look around after "Who calls?" and after "Bid every noise be still," and not go for the next sentence quite yet.

Budget problems affect productions of all kinds. The American Shakespeare Festival in Stratford, Connecticut, was housed in an immense theatre with a huge "thrust" stage with the audience seated about half the way around it. Shakespeare's plays received there some of their most elaborate productions in the United States. But because of financial exigencies, the festival theatre did not offer any season of plays in 1977. In 1973 the festival theatre revived for a second season the previous year's production of *Julius Caesar* with some changes in cast and settings. Wyman Pendleton, a professional actor of many years' standing, played the title role.

Wyman Pendleton on Figure 4:
I had played Caesar the season previously, but only for about a week or ten days, in the first version of this production in Connecticut. When the producing director turned it over for the next season to another director, the new man, in addition to questions of economics, wanted to have a different set of some sort. The first season we had been on this side of a half-mountain that we'd had to climb all through the production. So the second season we had this great oval. It completely changed the feeling of where we were. We were still in the same theatre, but this new production completely turned my head around on who Caesar was to be. The first season they had him as a sort of Hitler, but the second season I started off on the assumption that Caesar was a man who fully believed that he was right in everything he was doing. It wasn't blind ambition that made him decide to become emperor of the world. He believed those gods were around him. He was having them carried through the streets, their statues being put up. I didn't see that he was a villain at all or leading the world wildly astray. Of course, he was a man of im-

Figure 4. "Beware the Ides of March." Caesar faces the soothsayer, Act I, scene 2, American Shakespeare Festival, Stratford, Connecticut, 1973, with Wyman Pendleton as Caesar facing the soothsayer (Gene Nye). (Photo, Martha Swope.)

mense conceit, but then he had no awareness of that fact
whatsoever, of how other people looked at him. He loved
them all. He'd done this for them, he'd conquered that for
them.

I played the beginning of this scene as happy as a lark,
trying to make jokes. Then this person makes me annoyed
with his talk of the Ides of March. Caesar is annoyed to be
stopped, as though it just caught my attention for a
moment. Then I reacted as if I had the idea, "Let's get out
of here," and Caesar leaves, annoyed, angry, and a little
worry sitting on one shoulder. Caesar in our production
was a very superstitious person. The soothsayer in this
photograph, for instance, carries about those little amulets
and trinkets, and I, as Caesar, reacted to those respectfully.

Stan Singer, who is now a director in a university theatre
department, was a graduate student in theatre at the University of Kansas at Lawrence when he was cast in the role of
Mark Antony in *Julius Caesar* for the production in 1973
during the University's summer theatre festival. The theatre
in Lawrence is a regular auditorium except that the stage, as
Singer points out, is remarkably wide. Singer goes on to discuss how his interpretation of his role was influenced by
earlier interpretations and by the qualities of one of the
other actors in the same production.

Stan Singer on Figures 5 and 6:
This early scene shows how big a stage there is at Kansas,
a barn of a place. But scenes like this entrance of Caesar
[Fig. 5] or the soothsayer speaking [Fig. 6], though it is
obviously a posed picture, shows how well that stage can
work with big crowds like this.

People used to tell me that they liked the way Marlon
Brando did the role in the movie, but obviously I don't
look or talk like Marlon Brando. I had to act with my own
physical attributes, and to find a contrast to Brutus too.

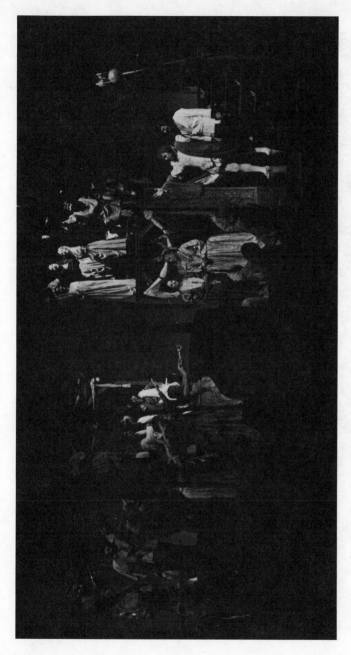

Figure 5. Caesar's triumphant entrance, Act I, scene 2, University of Kansas, 1973. At far right of picture is Caesar (David Cook) with Stan Singer as Mark Antony. (Photo, Andrew Tsubaki.)

17

Figure 6. "Beware the Ides of March." Caesar hears the soothsayer, Act I, scene 2, University of Kansas, 1973. (Photo, Andrew Tsubaki.)

I played Mark Antony as Caesar's protegé, his second in command, the youthful politician who did not know yet how to handle power, but who was always next to the man who did. When I was cast in the role, I was a little surprised, because Antony was historically short, stocky, and I'm tall and lean. The Brutus that we had was tall and lean, and a man with a poetic acting style, very good with language, so, since I couldn't offer a physical contrast, I tried this idea of the young executive, the young politician who came up, not because he'd been reared that way, like Octavius, but by being an athlete, a good runner.

Willam Kuhlke was the actor playing Brutus, with whom Singer sought, as Mark Antony, to contrast himself. Kuhlke was also one of Singer's teachers at Kansas, and is still a professor there. He too speaks of how he interpreted his role to keep it from looking too much like other earlier ones.

William Kuhlke on Figure 7:
In working on the role, I decided that I would have to combat the stereotypes that have grown up around the character of Brutus. He is not a villain, nor is he a copy-book hero. He's afflicted with a divided mind. He had high ambitions, and unimpeachable virtue, and yet, unfortunately, he cannot see himself for what he is, because he is also self-righteous. Another characteristic is moral vanity. He consistently thinks that he is doing the right thing for the right cause. And he is not a good judge of other men. He consistently makes crucial mistakes in his judgments of character. Yet he is not politically naive.

In this photograph, our Cassius is feeling me out about the possibility that Caesar might turn tyrant, and what we would do about that. Brutus here is aware of being wooed. But aware too of the danger in Caesar. Brutus doesn't care much for Cassius' insinuating manner at this point, and

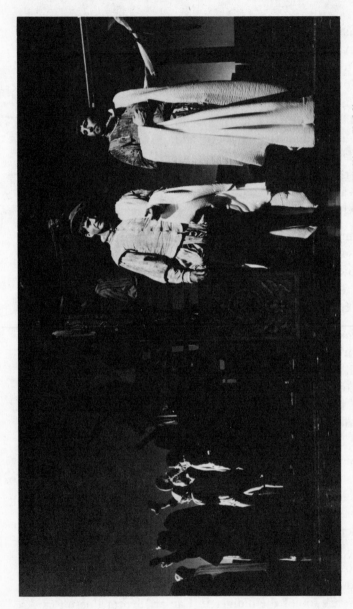

Figure 7. "Into what dangers would you lead me, Cassius?" William Kuhlke as Brutus speaks to Cassius (Fred Vesper), Act I, scene 2, University of Kansas, 1973. (Photo, Andrew Tsubaki.)

hates intrigue. He sees himself as pure of heart. He really believed it when he said to himself that there was no pride or ambition involved in his own motives. So the thought of some kind of intrigue is really distasteful to him. Then later on Casca comes in, a comic, rustic kind of character. Cassius and Casca played as if they were in league in this scene. Of course, I was never watching them when they revealed that.

The oldest Shakespeare festival in the United States is the one at Ashland, Oregon, begun by Angus Bowmer in the late thirties and perpetuated to this day largely by his efforts. The Oregon Shakespearean Festival has a loyal audience of long standing, and a tradition of producing plays by standards similar to those probable in Renaissance England during Shakespeare's lifetime. The company performs the plays completely uncut, without intermission, at an outdoor theatre and, especially in the early summer, begins the plays in broad daylight. The setting is a permanent background of Tudor style architecture behind a very wide and open stage platform, with two small covered areas, the "inner above" and the "inner below" at the center of the background.

The actors at Ashland are for the most part young people who have not yet joined the actors' union and are still official amateurs, though they may receive some small stipend for their summer's work at Ashland. Ric Hamilton had been at Ashland for several summers before he was cast in the role of Mark Antony in the summer of 1970. He has since become a professional actor on the West Coast. He speaks of how it felt to act on that stage in Ashland and also comments on a novel item—a staircase—that had been added to the stage that summer for the production of *Julius Caesar.*

Ric Hamilton on Figure 8:
I liked the light in the early part of the plays—they are

acted outdoors and they begin before sundown—because for me as the sun set the enchantment increased as the show went on. It seemed pretty ordinary to start out in daylight, as if to say, "Okay, we're actors; our revels now are started," but as the evening progressed, the fading light drew the audience in as it got darker around them, and focused their attention.

That stairwell at center stage drew a lot of comment. But I enjoyed the fact that it was there, even though it did dictate a lot of the movement on the stage. But as far as the speech for that funeral oration went, I was all for it.

Michael Winters, who now directs theatre at a California junior college, had been new as an actor at Ashland in the summer of 1970. He was cast then in the role of Casca, and he too comments on the staircase on that stage, and the apparent aims of that production of *Julius Caesar*.

Michael Winters on Figure 8:
The set had a big staircase in the middle of it. That's all the set there was. It was largely there for what the director considered the central sequence of the play, the funeral oration, so we had to work around it, and there were some difficulties in terms of sightlines. Otherwise it was a spare production, no messing with it, no little extra bits just because someone said, "Oh, I know what that means!"

Winters has an expressive voice and face. He recited some lines from the play in intonations and expressions imitative of ones famous from Watergate hearings then on television, pointing out that this sort of topical satire was never attempted in Oregon.

We stuck very close to what was implied in the text. And in fact the staircase caused a lot of furor, and not just with the patrons, but with the guys who ran the theatre. They

Figure 8. "Yond Cassius has a lean and hungry look." Caesar (Phil Davidson) speaks to Ric Hamilton as Mark Antony in the inner above while looking down at Cassius, played by Raye Birk, far left, and Brutus (Tom Donaldson); Ashland, Oregon, 1970. Directly behind Ric Hamilton is Michael Winters as Casca; next to him are Calpurnia (Candace Birk) and Cicero (Richard Yarnell). (Photo, Carolyn Mason-Jones.)

liked it to be the way it was in Shakespeare's day, and that staircase didn't seem to be traditional.

Raye Birk, who when interviewed for this book was starring in a play at the American Conservatory Theatre in San Francisco, played the role of Cassius at Ashland in 1970, and he too comments first on the staircase on the stage, and then speaks of the kind of influence space and ambiance can have on an interpretation of a role.

Raye Birk on Figure 8:
The idea behind the festival at Ashland is to do Shakespeare's plays as they might have been done in Shake-

speare's day on a stage like the one for which they were written. The people in charge, like Angus Bowmer, whose energy and dedication made that festival a reality, were always very specific about what they thought ought to be on that stage. As a result, there became a tradition on what to expect in terms of design and staging, and things didn't change much. They would change decorations, the banners, hang things from pillars, use the inner above and below because there is historical precedent for that, and use all the traps in the stage floor, but other than that, the actual architecture never changed much.

We argued for the stairs on the grounds that Shakespeare's text suggests that they get from the inner above to the inner below in the space of four lines, so there must have been some sort of stairs, backstage at least. But there's no scholarship to support the idea that they ever put such a staircase on the stage in Shakespeare's day. The design was approved, but did not really meet with the approval of the festival's tradition. But it was fun for the directors to have this new scenic element.

I remember that we rehearsed the first scene between Cassius and Brutus indoors because it rained so much that spring in Oregon. At Ashland, everything is usually rehearsed on the stage. Indoors we had found some interesting values in that scene, but when we moved outside to the big stage they seemed to disappear. There had been a quiet, conspiratorial contact between us. But outside, in front of twelve hundred people, it was only oratorical. We had to make some changes.

Wyman Pendleton, commenting on a photograph of a moment later on in Act I, has some further thoughts about his interpretation of Caesar's motives, and how the character seems to relate to others.

Wyman Pendleton on Figure 9:

Those lines of Mark Antony's about how Caesar put away the crown thrice . . . well, I'm not sure that I ever resolved in my own mind why Caesar did that, why he kept putting it away. Evidently it was too much for him, because he promptly had an epileptic fit!

When he comes into the scene with Brutus and Cassius and warns Antony against Cassius, as in this photograph, it is quite obvious that Caesar is suspicious of Cassius. As he sees Cassius, he's barely over the seizure that he'd had. Maybe he's somewhat jealous of Cassius. And he's afraid. This Cassius is the man he thinks is really striving to do him in or to take his place. He trusts Mark Antony. His other mistake, of course, is that he trusts Brutus too. But at that point in the play, he should trust Brutus, for Brutus still has not committed himself to Cassius and the others.

Michael Levin, another professional actor typical of those at the American Shakespeare Festival, played the role of Mark Antony in that same production with Pendleton in 1973. In his analysis of his role, he speaks, as modern actors often do, of the Orson Welles production in 1937.

Michael Levin on Figure 9:

I saw Antony in a very straight way. The death of Caesar is for him the death of a father-figure. Antony is the one in the play who is Caesar's heir. The theme of the play is the death of the father-king and the chaos that comes of that. So my Antony is not at all the Orson Welles fascist. There was a certain innocence to him. As the play opens, he has a cavalier attitude toward politics. He's having a ball in Rome. Caesar adores him. He is himself the number one young patrician in Caesar's group. He's not dumb.

Figure 9. "Would he were fatter—but I fear him not." Michael Levin as Mark Antony marks the words of Caesar, played by Wyman Pendleton, Act I, scene 2. American Shakespeare Festival, 1973. (Photo, Martha Swope.)

He knows that Cassius is not everybody's pal, but he tells Caesar not to worry about Cassius.

Another Caesar, Robert Prosky, also has some further comments on a photograph of roughly the same moment in the production at the Arena stage in 1974, mentioning the costumes and relationship of his character with others.

Prosky on Figure 10:
One of the greatest ways for anybody to find the movement of a specific period is to wear the clothes of the period. One moves differently in this gown that I'm wearing in this photograph than in modern street clothes. It had a huge purple overgarment. And the way that I'm sitting in this picture is dictated by the garment itself, the way it folds. You just don't sit the way you would sit in jeans. An actor can learn some of that from drawings of the period, but wearing the costume itself dictates it to him.

That's Mark Antony that I'm talking to, near the beginning of the play. The photographs suggest that extremely important relationship between Caesar and Mark Antony, almost a father-and-son relationship. And it suggests too Caesar's large view of himself.

Stanley Anderson played Mark Antony with Prosky at the Arena stage production of *Julius Caesar* in 1974. His reaction to the photograph of this moment in the play is very similar to Prosky's, commenting on the relationship between Caesar and Mark Antony.

Stanley Anderson on Figure 10:
We tried very hard in the three brief scenes that Caesar and Antony share to establish the "man-to-man" relationship between them as one of "father to wayward—but admired—son." We attempted to portray them as men of "sporting natures" who each acknowledge the others' flaws

Figure 10. "Fear him not, Caesar, . . . / He is a noble Roman, and well given." Stanley Anderson as Mark Antony reassures Robert Prosky as Caesar with Calpurnia (Leslie Cass), rear, Act I, scene 2, Arena Stage, 1974. (Photo, Alton Miller.)

Figure 11. "I saw Mark Antony offer him a crown." David Regal as Casca, seated, reports to Brutus (E. Lee Smith), left, and Cassius, played by Richard Greene, on what Caesar did in the Coliseum, Act I, scene 2, Hilberry Classic Theatre, 1968. (Photo, Wayne State University Photo Services.)

as well as attributes, and who as knowledgeable warriors prefer interesting peace to peaceful interests.

David Regal played Casca at the Hilberry Classic Theatre production in 1968. In terms reminiscent of those used by Prosky to discuss his interpretation of Caesar in connection with Figure 2, Regal describes some of the ways he found to make Casca seem psychologically consistent.

David Regal on Figure 11:
This scene with Brutus and Cassius here had as its whole tenor something that Greene, as Cassius, and I had worked out together. Cassius in this play was his own man, went his own way. So we used Casca's "It was Greek to me" as a feigned indifference, imitation by Casca of Cassius. Casca was a sycophant. He would do anything, play any game, and Cassius was the guy that Casca wanted to be affiliated with. That's how, as an actor, I justified Casca as the man who is first to stab Caesar later in the play.

Julius Caesar:
Act II

Raye Birk, playing Cassius at Ashland, comments on how the "orchard scene" of Act II contains within its text suggestions for the probable original blocking of Shakespeare's time. Then, as Ric Hamilton did in connection with Figure 8, Birk goes on to discuss what it was like to play that scene on the stage at Ashland.

Raye Birk on Figures 12 and 13:
This is the orchard scene. Clues as to how it should be staged and played are in the text, even down to where people are standing. The fact that we don't all come in at once reveals the conspiracy: these are proper Roman citizens, suddenly behaving like thugs. We emphasized that and immediately found solutions of who is speaking to whom and what they are talking about.

Some actors and directors at Ashland are strongly influenced by the time of evening in which the scene is played. In this photograph it is still daylight at that time of the summer. We had to suggest ways in which we are dealing with a darkness around us on the stage. Shakespeare's actors had the same problem as they performed the whole play in broad daylight.

And if the air is still warm, the actors have to work harder to be heard. And there's more distraction for the audience. But by the end of Act IV an actor can be fairly intimate and the sound will carry. But in the early scenes we had to work harder, and that work did detract from some of the values that we had discovered at rehearsals.

Michael Winters, in the role of Casca at Ashland, speaks

Figure 12. Brutus (Tom Donaldson), front right, in the orchard scene, Act II, scene 2, Oregon Shakespearean Festival, 1970, receives the conspirators: Casca, played by Michael Winters; Cinna (Christopher Leggette); Decius Brutus (John Arnone); Trebonius (John R. Darrah); in back, Metellus Cimber (Roger Kozol) and in front of him, Cassius, played by Raye Birk. (Photo, Carolyn Mason-Jones.)

Figure 13. "And for Mark Antony, think not of him." Brutus overrules Cassius, facing rear, in the orchard scene, Act II, scene 1, Oregon Shakespearean Festival, 1970. (Photo, Carolyn Mason-Jones.)

as if he felt, as actor, what the character Casca was apparently feeling, being left out while Cassius and Brutus whispered during the orchard scene.

Michael Winters on Figures 12 and 13:
Casca seems to take the place of many of the minor conspirators. The rest of them are rather undifferentiated by the text. In the orchard scene here, even he is undifferentiated, just along with the rest of them. We talked about where the sun would rise while Brutus and Cassius spoke aside with each other. No one used the line about the rising of the sun to point at Brutus. It was all very literal. I remember of course most clearly the two scenes in which I spoke a lot of lines, the first one with Cassius and Brutus, and then the one after the storm. The others, this one in the orchard, or coming to escort Caesar the next morning to the Senate, I felt more like just a spear-carrier.

John-Frederick Jones not only played Caesar in Maine in 1973; he also played Brutus at the Old Globe Theatre in Los Angeles in 1976. Here he speaks of the orchard scene in that Los Angeles production, reporting on several relationships between the characters and then on some of the technical details regarding delivery of certain speeches in that scene.

John-Frederick Jones on Figure 14:
The orchard scene, a wonderful scene. After Brutus has that soliloquy about killing Caesar—that is a little breathing moment in the tempo of the play—then the others come in and it's churning again. The conspirators were played as very unsure, scared, but factional too, because some were out for blood, wanted to kill everybody. But they were also played as a little intimidated of Brutus, because he's their social superior. So if Brutus wants to do it

Figure 14. "And for Mark Antony, think not of him." Brutus played by John-Frederick Jones, center, overrules Cassius (Frank Savino) left in the orchard scene, Act II, scene 1, Old Globe Theatre, Los Angeles, 1976. (Photo, Mitchell Rose.)

his way, they go along with it. When they want to swear
an oath, Brutus got a little angry that their mere state-
ments need an oath to keep them from breaking their
words. Shakespeare never has Brutus plead with them.
Brutus tells them, nearly commands them. He says he
won't have Cicero, because the younger conspirators want
to use Cicero's noble reputation as a shield to hide their
own responsibility for the killing. When I gave the line
about wanting to kill Caesar's spirit, but not Caesar, some
of the others in the scene turned to give me a look, as if
to say, "Wait a minute, you mean you don't want to go
through with it after all?" That's this photograph [Fig. 14].
Then Brutus goes on, "But alas, . . ." and the other actors
relax again. Here they are all pulling back, just little hub-
bub there, so that the line from Brutus "But alas, . . ." is
a reaction; the other actors onstage gave me an action for
that half of the speech to be reacting against.

Richard Greene, speaking of the orchard scene in which he
played Cassius at the Hilberry Classic Theatre in 1968, is
more concerned with his disappointment over the posed
quality of the photograph than he is with his memories of
how it felt to act that scene.

Greene on Figure 15:
This is one composed for the eye of the photographer;
ironically, one gets the impression that Brutus is adminis-
tering an oath. Of course, in Shakespeare's scene, just the
opposite is true. Brutus delivers a passionate discourse
against the need for swearing an oath. I look at these shots
and know how poorly they serve the event. It was a
Julius Caesar characterized by turbulence. Roman citizens swept through the theatre, overrunning the stage and
poured down the aisles. The vigor that dominated our production is not visible in these photographs.

Figure 15. "No, not an oath." Brutus (E. Lee Smith), with raised hand as center, overrules Cassius in the orchard scene, Act II, scene 1, Hilberry Classic Theatre, 1968. Clockwise after Brutus are Metellus Cimber (Fred Napier), Decius Brutus (Henry Hoffman), Trebonius (Fred Coffin), Cinna (John Sterling Arnold), David Regal as Casca and Richard Greene as Cassius. (Photo, Wayne State University Photo Service.)

Figure 16. "Cowards die many times before their deaths." Caesar, played by Robert Prosky, rejects the entreaties of Calpurnia (Leslie Cass), Act II, scene 2, Arena Stage, 1974. (Photo, Alton Miller.)

But David Regal, playing Casca in that scene at the Hilberry, responds with a report on some of the arrangements for characterization that had been made among the actors. Like Winters in connection with Figure 12 and 13, Regal mentions Casca's feeling of being left out.

David Regal on Figure 15:
This is the orchard scene, and it looks like Brutus is leading the pledge. But Greene as Cassius has just said, "Let us swear our resolution," and everybody else stuck out his hand too, as if to say, "Yeah, me too," and then Brutus says, "No, not an oath." Here it looks like he's leading it.

A lot of my action in the play was "me too" to Cassius. I was linked up with Cassius as his ally. There were very few times when I had to make a decision about the scene. I gave those eyeballs over toward Cassius and acted according to whatever Cassius was doing. So, as an actor too, I had to depend on what Greene was doing, but sometimes I couldn't.

When we talk about where the sun comes up in this scene, we tried for the tension of being left out, standing around. "What are Brutus and Cassius whispering about? What are we doing here if we're not included? What's going on?"

Robert Prosky as Caesar at the Arena Stage points out that a moment in Act II underlines some of the realities of acting that do not always get much consideration.

Robert Prosky on Figure 16:
In the Arena Stage, some members of the audience are quite close to the actors. Once in this scene here, with Calpurnia, I was sitting there up on that platform. We had a school matinee, and one little girl was sitting quite close to me. I was mouthing Shakespeare's lines in all

Figure 17. "Your wisdom is consum'd in confidence." Caesar, played by Wyman Pendleton, is convinced by Calpurnia (Grayce Grant) that he should stay at home, Act II, scene 2, American Shakespeare Festival, 1973. (Photo, Martha Swope.)

Figure 18. "This dream is all amiss interpreted." Decius Brutus (Alvah Stanley) convinces Caesar, played by Wyman Pendleton, to go to the Capitol after all, Act II, scene 2, American Shakespeare Festival, 1973. (Photo, Martha Swope.)

their glory, and, you know, when actors speak Shake-speare, they expectorate, they spit all over each other, something that the audience doesn't notice when the actors are on a stage and farther from them than in this arena. This little girl just looked up and said, quite loudly, "Stop spitting on me, Caesar!" One of the problems of working in the round.

Wyman Pendleton describes the same scene from the production of the play at the American Shakespeare Festival in 1973, emphasizing the way the scene works to provide Caesar's motivation.

Wyman Pendleton on Figure 17 and 18:
These two are of the scene in which Caesar is convinced that he ought to go to the Senate. Caesar is shown as a man divided against himself. And the entrance of Decius Brutus is perfect timing, on the part of Decius Brutus and on the part of Shakespeare too, of course. Ceasar has just been needled by his wife, and Caesar sees in himself a weakness that he had given in to her at all, in front of these men.

On the same scene, John-Frederick Jones, who played Caesar in Maine, comments critically on his own suitability for the role in which he was cast there, and then on the same scene at the Old Globe Theatre in Los Angeles, where he played Brutus. Then he returns to the topic in the background of many production problems: the budget.

John-Frederick Jones on Figures 19, 20, and 21:
This is another of those moments in playing Caesar in Maine when I felt too young. The point of the scene is to show how Caesar covets the crown. He allows his wife's pleading to deflect him because he's "superstitious grown of late," but when Decius says they will laugh at him—he turns and goes.

Figure 19. The senators call on Caesar, played by John-Frederick Jones, being helped into his robes, to escort him to the Capitol, Act II, scene 2. Among them at the rear are William Wright as Mark Antony, center; to his left, Brutus (John Fields); and Cassius (John Tormey), Cumston Hall, Monmouth, Maine, 1973. (Photo, Arthur Griffiths.)

Figure 20. John-Frederick Jones as Caesar, being arrayed to go to the Capitol, Act II, scene 2, watched from the rear by Brutus and Cassius, Monmouth, Maine, 1973. (Photo, Arthur Griffiths.)

Figure 21. John-Frederick Jones as Brutus comes to escort Caesar (Ed Knight), center, to the Capitol, Act II, scene 2, as Caesar speaks to Calpurnia (Karen McLaughlin), Old Globe Theatre, Los Angeles, 1976. (Photo, Mitchell Rose.)

The scene develops cross purposes. Caesar wants to go to be crowned; the conspirators come to greet him, but really to kill him. The audience has to get the feeling that Caesar commands too much personal awe from Rome.

Both productions, the one here where I played Caesar in Maine, and this one where I played Brutus in Los Angeles, slighted that need to make Caesar look imposing— not because they didn't know any better, they did—but because there just wasn't enough money for the additional actors and their costumes to make the point about Caesar's power.

Julius Caesar:
Act III

The assassination of Caesar is the moment to which everything in the play builds and from which all that follows in the play comes. It is, in addition, one of the most exciting moments in all Shakespeare's plays, and for the actors one of the most technically complex parts of the play. The actors must all work together, not merely to make the action seem realistic, but also to fulfill the symbolic quality of this central episode, as either a savage spectacle, or a ritual execution, or something in between.

The question of the budget always obtrudes, for it dictates how the blood of Caesar, in which the script commands the conspirators literally to wash their hands, will be shown on the stage. Even washable "blood" has to be washed out, and if there is no budget for laundering the costumes, or if the costumes cannot be washed and dried in time for a succeeding performance, or if the budget dictates reusing costumes from years ago that may not be as washable as the fake blood is, some other way of dealing with the blood will have to be invented.

John-Frederick Jones, who played Brutus at the Old Globe in Los Angeles in 1976 and Caesar at Cumston Hall in Monmouth, Maine, in 1973, comments on the differences in the two ways that the assassinations were organized in those two productions.

John-Frederick Jones on Figures 22 through 27:
Here's the assassination scene. Here in Los Angeles we all went in on Caesar at the same time. The characters' reasons for talking to Caesar in these first photographs of the

47

Figure 22. "Metellus Cimber throws before thy seat / An humble heart." Caesar (Ed Knight), seated, hears a petition. Kneeling is Cimber (Ed Harris); center is Cinna (Ludwig Bonenberg). To the right is Ligarius (Pat Tercelle) and, as Brutus, John-Frederick Jones, Act III, scene 1 the assassination scene, Old Globe Theatre, Los Angeles, 1974. (Photo, Mitchell Rose.)

Figure 23. "Is there no voice more worthy than my own?" Metellus Cimber (Ed Harris) turns to the other conspirators for help with his appeal to Caesar (Ed Knight). Left is Casca (Rob Curtin), and in the rear a servant and Cassius (Frank Savino), Act III, scene 1, Old Globe Theatre, Los Angeles, 1974. (Photo, Mitchell Rose.)

Figure 24. "I am constant as the northern star." Casca (Rob Curtin), left foreground, listens to Caesar (Ed Knight) reject the suit of Metellus Cimber (Ed Harris), Act II, scene 1, Old Globe Theatre, Los Angeles, 1974. (Photo, Mitchell Rose.)

Figure 25. At the Old Globe Theatre in Los Angeles, Act III, scene 1, 1974, the conspirators all pull their daggers out. Left to right, Casca (Rob Curtin), Cassius (Frank Savino), Cinna (Ludwig Bonenberg), Caesar (Ed Knight), and Ligarius (Pat Torelle). (Photo, Mitchell Rose.)

Figure 26. A quiet moment: Brutus, played by John-Frederick Jones, stands over the body of Caesar, Act III, scene 1, Old Globe, Los Angeles, 1974. (Photo, Mitchell Rose.)

production in Los Angeles are to get close to him, but on this little stage we were already close, milling around. Then after we stabbed him, one of the others threw a cloak over the actor Caesar. That hid the lack of blood. We didn't do that in Maine, but then in Maine we had plenty of blood.

Here in Los Angeles we put the line, "Et tu, Brute?" in before the stabbing, at a point when Caesar could see that I—that is, Brutus—was with the rest of the conspirators, with their knives out. He had tried to get out, one way, but someone was there, and then another, until the only way offstage open to him was the one that Brutus was standing in. He said, "Et tu, Brute?" and then I turned toward him and drew my sword, and that was the signal. We all rushed in upon him.

The normal business is for each conspirator to do it one at a time, as we did when I played Caesar in Maine. I struggled downstage right after everyone but Brutus had stabbed me, with the blood capsule in my mouth, and Brutus then had this private moment with me just before he stabbed me too.

The play has been building to the moment. That's why Shakespeare has the business afterward of the washing of the hands in blood, to spread it around even more. Here in Los Angeles we did not have the budget to launder the costumes. We had only these costumes and one for each actor. In Monmouth, of course, I wore that pre-bloodied robe. In Los Angeles, during rehearsals, I hinted at the idea that we had used in Monmouth, but we had such a problem with it that the director finally resolved it another way by going to red light. During the assassination scene we had all red lighting on the stage, and it all combined stylistically, so that when the normal colored lights came up again, the red was gone, and we didn't have to deal with

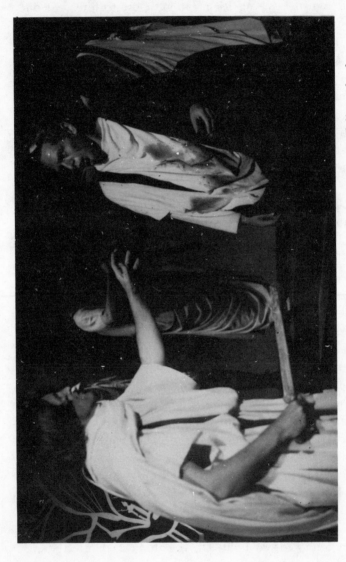

Figure 27. "Et tu, Brute?" Brutus (John Fields) prepares to deliver the last blow to Caesar, played by John-Frederick Jones, Monmouth, Maine, 1973. (Photo, Arthur Griffiths.)

it. It worked well for our audiences here in Los Angeles, though a squeamish effect from lots of blood would be legitimate too. We had worked for that in Maine, where we also used a red wash light to disguise the pre-bloodied robe. Both directors came up with the same idea independently.

Earl McCarroll, then as now teacher of theatre and speech at Ithaca College in Ithaca, New York, was the director in Maine that summer of 1973 for the production of *Julius Caesar* with Jones in the title role. He discusses more fully the way he found to make that assassination scene a part of his "concept" for the significance of the production.

Earl McCarroll on Figure 27:
One difficulty is the assassination itself, especially for a small repertory company such as this one in Maine, on a small budget. It is impossible to clean all those white togas after every performance. That immediately eliminates the idea of some kind of blood setup, squirting blood all over everybody. Even as we finally did it, we got some blood on somebody every night. The solution that I found came out of a concept that I had for the play as a whole. It seemed to me that we were, in this play, in the back rooms of the political situation, the smoke-filled rooms, so to speak. The play goes back and forth between the public and the private part of politics. Out of that came the idea of reversing the scene and having it played upstage. Caesar spoke with his back to the audience, upstage, facing the blue sky cyclorama at the back of the stage, while the downstage area, filled with the conspirators, was dim. Caesar could then enter wearing a bloodied robe with the stab marks already in it which in silhouette the audience could not see. The conspirators had swords that were already bloodied; it could not be seen that they were until the lights came up. It was an exciting perspective of the

Figure 28. "Et tu, Brute?" In the Hilberry Clissic Theatre production in 1968, Act III, scene 1, Brutus (E. Lee Smith) kneels to deliver the final blow to Caesar (Jeff Tambor). Others are, front, kneeling, Richard Greene as Cassius, and from left to right, Ligarius (Arthur Laupus) holding Popilius Lena (Jeff Rodman); Trebonius (Fred Coffin); Publius (Robert Larsen); David Regal as Casca; Decius Brutus (Henry Hoffman); Cinna (John Sterling Arnold); and Metellus Cimber (John Napier). (Photo, Wayne State University Photo Services.)

scene. It did come out of necessity, the laundry problem, but it was a more exciting way of approaching the scene than the traditional. And it isolated Brutus. His is the most important, the most dramatic decision. We had him move down right, alone there in natural light, and then on the moment that he stabbed Caesar the natural light for the whole stage came up, revealing the blood on the swords and the gashes and blood on Caesar's toga, as he pulled away from Brutus, bit the bloodbag in his mouth, and fell toward the audience.

The assassination scene in *Julius Caesar* at the Hilberry Classic Theatre at Wayne State University in Detroit in 1968 shows another solution, more elaborate than McCarroll's in Maine in 1973. One of the actors at the Hilberry, Richard Greene in the role of Cassius, describes the scene at first somewhat analytically, but later he begins to describe how much fun it was.

Richard Greene on Figure 28:
In the assassination scene at the Hilberry, Caesar did not fight back. Once he knew what was happening, he accepted, even embraced the blows. It was an execution that began as ritual but exploded into chaos.

I think that the togas should have been white. It's a strong symbol. There's that constant talk about honor, about how these men are an elite group. They should be in white togas. It may be impractical from a laundry point of view, but some extravagance is necessary to make a statement.

You see in this photograph that we wore special overgarments. They were a grey, wash-and-wear fabric. They concealed our individual blood sacs and daggers, and gave us something to wipe all that gore on. After the scene we dropped our assassination togas into the wash bin. In this photograph, they look like big dinner napkins, don't they?

We used blood in an enema bag hidden under one of the conspirators' toga. He would kneel downstage of Caesar's body with his back to the audience and unload a great pool of blood all over Caesar's chest. This was easily masked at the Hilberry because that auditorium has no audience in a balcony overlooking the stage.

After Caesar was down, and Brutus said, "Stoop and wash," we all went into a huddle over the body, squirted that blood around over hands and arms, and it was messy. I got so grossly carried away as actually to drink Caesar's blood. There was some running down my jaw as I proclaimed, ". . . So often shall the knot of us be call'd / The men that gave their country liberty." Our shoes seemed poorly designed. When the blood started to flow, the stage floor became as slippery as ice. Our smooth, flat leather soles didn't help. More than once an actor lost his balance. Also, the shoe was open at the toes. With all those heavy metal blades flying, that was an invitation for injury.

David Regal, who played Casca at the Hilberry Classic Theatre production in 1968, describes how the technical aspects of this scene in that production were a product of the concept for the play as a whole. Then he goes into more technical matters. He too mentions how slippery the blood was and describes his own progress through the assassination scene to the moment shown in this photograph.

David Regal on Figure 28:
The concept for this production was simply, "Let's tell the story," and had a goal of satisfying the high school audiences to which the Hilberry plays a lot of its Shakespeare. So we had blood and guts abounding. This pillar here, with the waffle-marks, oozed blood in the assassination scene. Those spaghetti westerns were just first being shown about then, and we were going to outdo them.

The blood we used in the assassination was a kind of pudding with a red dye in it, like instant pudding that never set. Slippery on the stage? Murder! On these little steps someone was always taking a dive. It was blocked mechanically, "You go that way, then go this way, then if you get out of his way, he can come over and get him in the gut, then that one can stab him in the back," but the reality of it for the actors came alive when all of us were slithering around in all that blood, nearly falling off the stage, barely able to make a thrust. That vitality was restored by the chaos, the butchery of that scene.

The whole crowd started out standing around, setting Caesar up. I started here, about where Greene is now in this photograph. I worked my way up the stairs while Caesar was talking, where I gave Caesar the first blow. All the time there was just as much chance for me to back out and call it off as there was to do it. Lots of eyeballing then. All the other guys had their backs to the audience, listening to Caesar, eyeballing me, and waiting for me. We stretched it, like maybe I wasn't going to do it. With the decision to hit Caesar, the last bit of whatever ties Casca to the human process goes. Pretty soon he's threatening everybody with his knife. The kind of schizoid thing I was working for was that as soon as Casca feels the blood on his hands, he becomes the real dangerous killer. Here's a guy who wants to go on our side, but Casca's not listening; he's put a knife in the guy's face.

The production of *Julius Caesar* at the University of Kansas in the summer of 1973 played to an auditorium without a balcony, so that as Greene pointed out for the production at the Hilberry in connection with Figure 28, certain standard practices for showing blood on stage could be used. William Kuhlke, who played Brutus at Kansas, describes the assassination there.

William Kuhlke on Figure 29:
Caesar had to be assassinated, that much was clear to Brutus. And he had wanted the conspirators to do it in such a fashion that they all shared the onerous task.

Caesar was struck by several people first, starting with Casca, then he reeled from the stage left to stage right, and each stabbed him in succession. Finally in his progress he wheeled downstage right, where I waited for him. In his eyes was pain, wonder, and when he looked at me, a question, expecting help. It's a terrible moment for Brutus, one in which he confronts the realities of the act which his ideals have led him to espouse. And so he plunges the dagger in. Caesar hangs over his shoulder. Then I pushed him away, stood there as he fell.

The blood came from blood capsules. After Caesar fell, we gathered around the body, and at that point we bathed our hands in blood—we passed the capsules around, broke the capsules, bathed our hands—and then rose up over his body, in a ritual way, our hands streaming blood.

Stan Singer, who played Mark Antony at Kansas, and was therefore not even onstage during the assassination scene, can nevertheless add some more technical details to the ways in which the effect of stabbings on Caesar's clothing were accomplished at Kansas.

Stan Singer on Figure 29:
Caesar had two linings in his toga. As the conspirators came up on him and circled around him, their knives were going up. They grabbed him, tore at his toga, and turned it over, then they draped it back on him. On the inside lining all those holes showed in it. Whe he fell, his toga had just been turned inside out. As the conspirators were stabbing him, they took little blood capsules, popped them over in their hands—and tried to keep the blood off their costumes.

Figure 29. "Et tu, Brute?" Brutus played by William Kuhlke, about to deliver the final blow to Caesar (David Cook), Act III, scene 1, University of Kansas, 1973. (Photo, Andrew Tsubaki.

Wyman Pendleton, Caesar at the production at the American Shakespeare Festival, describes the assassination on a stage so huge and before an audience so big, and able to see the action from so many different angles, that the application of blood after the assassination was all over would not have been effective. Furthermore, at the American Shakespeare Festival, the budget did not much affect the way the assassination was staged.

Wyman Pendleton on Figures 30 through 37:
I rather liked our assassination in Connecticut. I moved from murderer to murderer. First, here I am up from the throne and out, people are kneeling, and I am giving the lines about how I am the north star. Then Casca, there, comes from behind. His blow made me stagger forward, and here another, and there it is Cassius. His blow would spin me. Brutus was down right. I did a full turn, and I had a blood capsule to slap against my chest, then said, "Et tu, Brute?" having just bitten a second capsule, so that it would drizzle while I was saying it, and then Brutus would catch me in a circle of his arms. I did a back bend out of his arms and slid head first down the steps and flopped, and as long as my feet didn't bounce, it worked.

For the blood we had in the wardrobe two complete sets of costumes, and they just washed them over and over. The blood was some vegetable dye that comes right out. Though once or twice the costumes didn't get quite dry, and when we did the play two times in one day, I put on some pretty wet costumes.

The main difficulty is breathing when one has just died, just to catch the breath. I used to die with my eyes open. Mark Antony would close them. Fairly quickly. I got to know all the lights in the ceiling. I had one that I would stare at, just to the right of the bulb.

Figure 30. "I am constant as the northern star." The assassination scene, Act III, scene 1, American Shakespeare Festival, 1973. Cinna (Philip Taylor), left, Brutus (Philip Kerr), and Decius Brutus (Alvah Stanley) plead with Wyman Pendleton in the role of Caesar, as Cassius (Lee Richardson) and Metellus Cimber (Theodore Sorel) kneel at right. (Photo, Martha Swope.)

Figure 31. "Doth not Brutus bootless kneel?" Caesar refuses even Brutus as Decius Brutus looks over to see Casca (Rex Everhart) just coming into the picture with his dagger drawn. (Photo, Martha Swope.)

Figure 32. The conspirators draw their daggers. From left are Brutus, a senator, and Cinna. Decius Brutus prepares to strike as Wyman Pendleton in the role of Caesar whirls on Casca, who is drawing back after striking. In front, Cassius draws his dagger and Metellus Cimber threatens three other senators. (Photo, Martha Swope.)

Figure 33. Decius Brutus strikes at Caesar; Casca whirls on the surrounding crowd, as Metellus Cimber turns from the crowd to run at Caesar. (Photo, Martha Swope.)

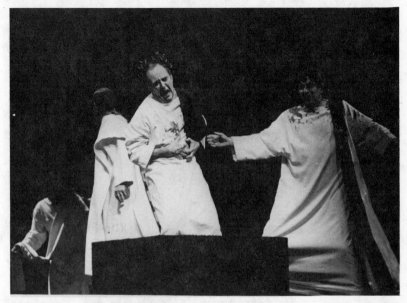

Figure 34. Casca holds back the senators as Caesar staggers away from a blow by Cassius. (Photo, Martha Swope.)

Figure 35. "Et tu, Brute?" Brutus, left prepares to give the final blow, while Metellus Cimber, center, looks over his shoulder to watch Caesar, played by Wyman Pendelton, running toward Brutus. (Photo, Martha Swope.)

Figure 36. After striking Brutus kneels to catch the body of Caesar, played by Wyman Pendleton. (Photo, Martha Swope.)

Figure 37. Brutus (Philip Kerr) lowers the dying Caesar, played by Wyman Pendleton, to the floor, Act III, scene 1, American Shakespeare Festival, 1973. (Photo, Martha Swope.)

At the Oregon Shakespearean Festival, the staircase that had been introduced onto the stage for the production of *Julius Caesar* in 1970 demanded to be used for the assassination. Raye Birk, who played Cassius, describes in general how the action was organized on the stairway.

Raye Birk on Figures 38 through 50:
We did the assassination all the way down the stairs. Casca stabbed Caesar first up here, and then he was handed down, and everyone got a shot at him, and finally he fell the last few steps. I was up here on the first landing, and Brutus was at the bottom. Caesar sprawled coming down the stairs, never falling. He was being handled. It took a lot of rehearsals to get that right. Some of it was hard because of the turn we had to do at the landing. There was no hand rail. Negotiating that turn was very tricky for the actor playing Caesar and for everyone else. We had to catch him. He fell to us. And we didn't dare step back because we could step right off the platform. The costumes, which I remember liking, had capes that made this difficult too, because we'd be backing down the stairs and would step on the hem of the cape. After we got Caesar turned, he went down the last steps, faced Brutus, said, "Et tu, Brute?" and covered his face.

Casca is the one who delivers the first blow. Michael Winters played the role at Ashland. In terms reminiscent of David Regal's comments in connection with Figure 28, Winters describes how he got into position to deliver the blow, and then how the assassination went after that.

Michael Winters on Figures 38 through 50:
I spent the early part of the scene as one of the conspirators at the foot of the stairs, then worked my way up to the top to get behind Caesar. The assassination started here, on "Speak, hands, for me," at the top of the stairs, and then

Figure 38. "Casca, be sudden, for we fear prevention." The assassination scene, Act III, scene 1, Oregon Shakespearean Festival, Ashland, Oregon, 1970. At top center, Caesar (Phil Davidson) and Cicero (Richard Yarnell) listen to Popilius Lena (Loyd Williamson), nervously watched from below, left, by Ligarius (Rick Newman) while Decius Brutus (John Arnone) speaks to Casca, played by Michael Winters. Cinna (Christopher Leggette), lower right, looks on. On the stairs, Metellus Cimber (Roger Kozol) prepares to make his plea to Caesar, while Trebonius (John R. Darrah) begins to draw Mark Antony, played by Ric Hamilton, aside. (Photo, Carolyn Mason-Jones.)

Figure 39. "Know, Caesar doth not wrong." Caesar, watched by some senators, among them Popilius Lena and Cicero, above, rebuffs the kneeling Metellus Cimber; Michael Winters as Casca has reached the landing on the stairs beside Metellus Cimber; coming up the stairs from below is Ligarius. On the stage level, Raye Birk as Cassius and Brutus (Tom Donaldson) look at the nervous Decius Brutus; Cinna, right, continues to watch. (Photo, Carolyn Mason-Jones.)

Figure 40. "I kiss thy hand, but not in flattery." Brutus joins in the pleas on behalf of Metellus Cimber's suit, as Raye Birk in the role of Cassius comes up the stairs to joint Ligarius, Metellus Cimber, and Casca on the landing, while Popilius Lena, Caesar, and Cicero, all above, look on. (Photo, Carolyn Mason-Jones.)

Figure 41. "I am constant as the northern star," Caesar still rejects the suit. Cicero has moved away from Caesar, up three steps and into inner above, while Michael Winters as Casca has moved up to Caesar's level from the landing; Metellus Cimber, Raye Birk as Cassius, and Ligarius are all closer too, while Brutus is preparing to descend again. (Photo, Carolyn Mason-Jones.)

Figure 42. "Doth not Brutus bootless kneel?" Caesar rejects the pleas of both Cinna and Decius Brutus, bottom, while looking down at Brutus, now back on the stage floor out of the picture, as Casca raises his dagger to strike. Cicero has momentarily looked away, but Metellus Cimber, Cassius, and Ligarius all look on directly. (Photo, Carolyn Mason-Jones.)

Figure 43. "Speak, hands, for me," Michael Winters as Casca strikes Caesar from behind; Cicero, right, is horrified, while below, Metellus Cimber, Raye Birk as Cassius, Ligarius, and below them, Cinna on the left and Decius Brutus on the right, all draw their daggers. (Photo, Carolyn Mason-Jones.)

Figure 44. The senators back away from the threatening dagger held by Michael Winters as Casca and Cicero gapes on while Caesar (below Cicero) staggers down the steps to the waiting Metellus Cimber, Decius Brutus, Raye Birk in the role of Cassius, Ligarius, and, below them, Cinna. (Photo, Carolyn Mason-Jones.)

Figure 45. A senator and Cicero motion helplessly; Michael Winters as Casca looks down on Metellus Cimber stabbing Caesar, who has disappeared among the other four conspirators and their daggers; Cinna, Decius Brutus, Cassius, and Ligarius. (Photo, Carolyn Mason-Jones.)

Figure 46. "Et tu, Brute?" Brutus at the bottom of the stairs waits for the wounded Caesar to come down to him, while on the landing Cinna, Ligarius, Cassius, and Decius Brutus watch. (Photo, Carolyn Mason-Jones.)

Figure 47. Brutus thrusts his dagger into Caesar. Cinna, Ligarius, Cassius, and Decius Brutus, up on the stairs, watch. (Photo, Carolyn Mason-Jones.)

Figure 48. Brutus steps back to catch the dying Caesar's body. (Photo, Carolyn Mason-Jones.)

Figure 49. Brutus catches Caesar's body. (Photo, Carolyn Mason-Jones.)

Figure 50. "Liberty, Freedom! Tyranny is dead!" Cinna cries out as Brutus lowers the body of Caesar to the floor. Raye Birk in the role of Cassius leads the others down the stairs. (Photo. Carolyn Mason-Jones.)

Figure 51. "Let us bathe our hands in Caesar's blood." Cinna watches as Brutus raises the hand of Raye Birk in the role of Cassius. Michael Winters as Casca is kneeling by the body. Decius Brutus and Ligarius turn to listen. Trebonius, having just come back from getting Mark Antony away from the Capitol, comes over to look at the body. (Photo, Carolyn Mason-Jones.)

Caesar came down the steps, handed on from knife to knife, so that he could get to a spot on the stairs where one conspirator was waiting, and down to the next spot—which all that working our way up the stairs had helped to organize. After I hit him at the top there, he fell down to the next person, and the next, and then to somebody else. Then the last flight, and he came down right to Brutus.

Once again, as at Kansas and at the Hilberry Classic Theatre, because there is no balcony overlooking the action at Ashland, it was possible to arrange to display the blood after the assassination was over, as Winters describes.

Michael Winters on Figure 51:
After Caesar was lying on the stage, we all used little blood packs, and because of the laundry problem, Caesar was never bloodied, not during the assassination. His costume was silvery white with a purple or deep red cape over it. There was no way that they could bloody that and then clean it time after time. They made another costume for him and bloodied that one, so when he was carried on for the funeral scene, he was bloody. During this scene, meanwhile, we came on with the blood packs on strings hung on our fingers. Then we would go through the violence, then come down the steps, undo our sleeves, roll them up, and smear blood on our hands. As we made this huddle around the corpse here, we broke the blood bags, smeared the blood on the hands. Then this lifting of the hands, Brutus and Cassius, was the cue. Next we all turned so that it was revealed to the audience that we all had bloody hands.

Next Winters goes on to describe how a moment in one rehearsal had a lasting effect on succeeding performances of the immediate aftermath of the assassination.

Figure 52. "O mighty Caesar, dost thôu lie so low?" Decius Brutus, Brutus, Cinna, and Casca played by Michael Winters watch Ric Hamilton as Mark Antony come to see the body of Caesar. (Photo, Carolyn Mason-Jones.)

Figure 53. "Are all thy conquests, glories, triumphs, spoils, / Shrunk to this little measure?" Decius Brutus, Brutus, Cinna, and Casca (Michael Winters) watch Mark Antony (Ric Hamilton) stoop to the body of Caesar. (Photo, Carolyn Mason-Jones.)

Figure 54. "I know not . . . / Who else must be let blood . . . / If I myself, there is no hour so fit / As Caesar's death's hour." Brutus, Cinna, and Casca (Michael Winters) watch Mark Antony over the body of Caesar, while at right, Trebonius and Cassius (Raye Birk) also look on. (Photo, Carolyn Mason-Jones.)

Michael Winters on Figures 52, 53, and 54:
One thing that happened in rehearsal, and it scared me to death—it was my first season there, I hadn't worked as an actor in four years before I came there—we were in rehearsal for this scene one day, over the body. Ric Hamilton as Mark Antony was leaning over the body, and next he'd talk to us before we left the stage. We were just in rehearsal. It was one of those moments when an actor says to himself, "Yes, this is where I am, I stand here, and just listen to him." None of us were really tuned in.

Ric came up out of his speech and suddenly he was moving at me. He grabbed my sword away from me and turned it on me! And then he said, "Come on, you guys, get with it! I am very likely to take you all on!" From then on everybody paid a lot of attention to him! That scene always had an extra burst when we performed it.

Ric Hamilton's comments on the role of Mark Antony at Ashland concentrate on a problem in characterization that affects a number of other characters in *Julius Caesar,* the feeling that he is a person of two minds, of two conflicting personalities.

Ric Hamilton on Figures 52 through 57:
There was a problem in the scene right after the assassination for me with that staircase and the sightlines. The staircase got in the way of something I wanted to do in the role. After the conspirators have murdered Caesar, I wanted Antony to come in and survey the scene, and then back off. And then to come back in again. And I did that, but because of the staircase, the stage right fourth of the house could not see me. So it was a sort of secret that I shared with the other three-fourths of the house.

That whole scene with the conspirators was a huge problem for me because I didn't want Antony to be like a conspirator. He is. The play dictates that. But I wanted him to be a little more honest about it. It's very easy to walk in among the conspirators and indicate a faked friendship to them, all that—that's a very obvious choice to make.

By the time the first performance came along, I was trying in that scene to walk a tightrope between Antony's being conscious of what he had to do and of what he felt. Antony knew what had happened before he came onstage, and at the same time he is overcome by the sight of his

Figure 55. "O Antony, beg not your death of us." Brutus insists he means no harm. From left are Brutus, Cinna, Casca (Michael Winters), Mark Antony (Ric Hamilton) by Caesar's body, Cassius (Raye Birk), and Trebonius. (Photo, Carolyn Mason-Jones.)

Figure 56. "Let each man render me his bloody hand, / First, Marcus Brutus, let me shake with you." Brutus shakes hands with Mark Antony (Ric Hamilton) over the body of Caesar, while Decius Brutus, Cinna, Casca (Michael Winters), Cassius (Raye Birk), and Trebonius watch. (Photo, Carolyn Mason-Jones.)

Figure 57. "O, pardon me, thou bleeding piece of earth." Ric Hamilton as Mark Antony alone with the body of Caesar near the end of Act III, scene 1, Oregon Shakespearean Festival, 1970. (Photo, Carolyn Mason-Jones.)

friend, dead. In the first part of the play, Antony is the kind of person that power just comes to; the opportunity to be ruler of the world just comes to him, and he seizes that. He does become opportunistic for a period, but in the end, the power in the heart dominates the power in his mind.

The most important speech in the play for the actor playing Mark Antony is one that I don't think I was successful at, while he's talking to the body of Caesar while the conspirators are still there. That speech, and then the one he gives over the body after the conspirators have all gone off, those two are the crux for that character. Everything he does after that is determined by that scene.

The second of those, "O, bleeding piece of earth," I did

better with. It is very tempting to an actor. He is alone on
stage. It's hard not to wallow in it. I tried to take too
much time with it at first, and for a long time I couldn't
feel Antony's loss. Then later I experienced something in
my own life that I was able to use as the loss factor, to
place that speech where I wanted it. And then it gave me
a thrusting point for the rest of the role in the rest of the
play.

A contrast to Hamilton's analysis in method is William
Wright's discussion, entirely in terms of technique, of how
he played the same scene on the tiny stage at Cumston Hall
in Monmouth, Maine.

William Wright on Figure 58:
This is the moment I came on stage to see for myself what
the messenger had relayed: the dead and bleeding body of
Caesar. I played the scene as an Antony overwhelmed at
his friend's death, so moved that he thinks of nothing else,
even to the point of ignoring the conspirators and their
threat to Antony's own life. In this production, all conspirators remained on stage to view Antony's reaction.

Later, when it was time to shake hands with the conspirators, I didn't show any duplicity. In that little theatre
in Maine, to register too much would have caused the
audience to wonder why the conspirators hadn't noticed
Antony's "acting" a show of friendship. The conspirators
were roughly in a parallel line from upstage right to downstage left and I went from one to the next, registering
chagrin at Brutus, nothing with the others, until coming
to Cassius—the obvious one who would have been in any
conspiratorial group. With him I shook hands in a sar-
donic tone. With Casca I underscored the line "Valiant
Casca" giving a pause between the two words. I looked at
him before speaking and then held my hand out quickly,

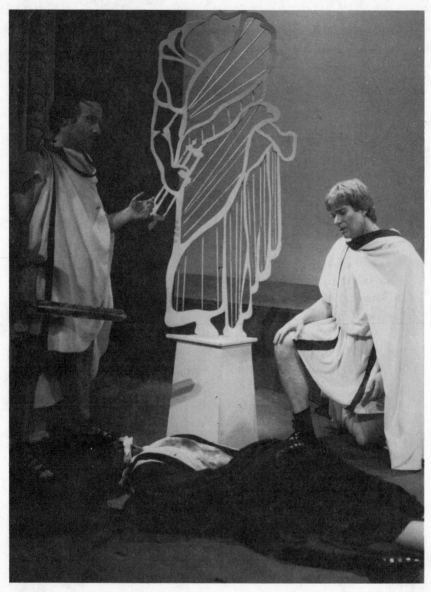

Figure 58. "O mighty Caesar, dost thou lie so low?" A conspirator stands over the body of Caesar (John-Frederick Jones) as William Wright in the role of Mark Antony sees it, Act III, scene 1, Monmouth, Maine, 1973. (Photo, Arthur Griffiths.)

startling him in fear. I held his hand just too long, looked him in the eye for an uncomfortable time, knowing him to be squirming inside his cowardly self. Anything more than those revelations of Antony's contempt would have been too much in that little theatre.

In describing the same moment in the play from the point of view of Brutus, John-Frederick Jones, who played Brutus at the Old Globe in Los Angeles, discusses some of the general issues of developing any character in ways similar to those employed by Prosky in connection with Figure 2 and Regal with Figure 11.

John-Frederick Jones on Figures 59 and 60:
Right after the assassination, both in the production in Maine and in this one in Los Angeles, there was this hush, as if the world seemed for a moment to stand still, and then, pandemonium, people running around. In Maine the conspirators were a little more steady, but in Los Angeles we had all the conspirators but Brutus go to pieces, get scared, call "Stand fast together" one made as if to guard the doors, to try to keep people out. That gave me as Brutus something to react against, so that Brutus can make again that point he always does, that the conspirators have nothing to apologize for. That became then Brutus' motive for having them all dip their hands in blood, to galvanize these terrified conspirators, to bring them back together again.

This photograph here [Fig. 59], that's our Mark Antony in Los Angeles, just after he's walked in among the conspirators. And here [Fig. 60] he's having his little quarrel with Cassius, when Cassius asks him, "What compact mean you to have with us?" It's danger time. Then Brutus, well, Brutus doesn't interrupt it, but Shakespeare arranges it so that the conversation comes back to Brutus, on "or else this were a savage spectacle."

Figure 59. "Let each man render me his bloody hand." Mark Antony (William Gunther) offers the gesture of conciliation to John-Frederick Jones as Brutus, Act III, scene 1, Old Globe Theatre, Los Angeles, 1976. (Photo, Mitchell Rose.)

Figure 60. "I blame you not for praising Caesar so, / But what compact mean you to have with us?" Cassius (Frank Savino), right, questions the motives of Mark Antony (William Gunther), by the body of Caesar. Left is Casca (Rob Curtin); center, back to camera, John-Frederick Jones as Brutus; and rear, Trebonius (Allan Stone). Act III, scene 1, Old Globe Theatre, Los Angeles, 1976. (Photo, Mitchell Rose.)

Earlier in this scene there's a speech that Brutus gives to Mark Antony, "beg not your death of us," that is another good example of those speeches Brutus has with a preface in it, one that makes other characters wait to see what he is really going to say. Back in that orchard scene [Figure 14], there was that moment when all the conspirators heard Brutus wish that they didn't have to kill Caesar, one that our actors played as if they thought that maybe Brutus was going to try to talk them out of it. Here Mark Antony and the conspirators have to wait and wait to see what it is that Brutus is finally going to say, until he gets to "For your part. . . ." That's the part of the speech that gives to Mark Antony the information that he has been made to wait for. This use of a preface to a speech often adds tension since it delays the statement of purpose on which action can be taken.

It's another of Brutus' mistakes, though, of course, an actor of Brutus cannot play a mistake! Cassius thinks it is; he doesn't want Antony to speak in the Forum. But Brutus says that he will settle everything by speaking first. He really shouldn't have let Mark Antony speak, but there's no way an actor can play a negative thing like a mistake. He has to play his character's purpose. The members of the audience, if they can bring themselves to agree with anything said by Cassius, might see it as a mistake, but the actor playing Brutus cannot play it that way.

Like Ric Hamilton at Ashland, Michael Levin, who played Mark Antony at the American Shakespeare Festival in Connecticut in 1973, speaks of the interior workings of the character's personality, and like Wright in the same role at Monmouth, Maine, Levin describes some of the technical details of his performance. In looking at the photographs he is also struck, like many of the actors in this book, by the costumes.

Michael Levin on Figures 61 through 65:

I took it as my subtext that Antony, when he hears of Caesar's death, is stunned. And that appearance, when he knows that Caesar is dead, I took as a rash move. As it turned out, it was politically effective, but to go in there, when they'd just killed Caesar, and he next in line. . . . He didn't have to go in there. It was just reckless to do that. He might have even harbored thoughts of revenge at that very moment. The other actors in the scene played it as if I might. In the speech over the body, I wept. I had had an experience with my own father, so it wasn't hard to find the emotion. And I played the whole scene, when he weeps over the body, and then when he talks to Brutus and to Cassius, and shakes hands, as if there were some question over whether he could control himself.

My Antony did not shake hands sincerely with them. He made a decision in there that this is the game we play right now, but later. . . . As soon as he looks up from the body, Antony decides to kill every one of them. He'd like to do it right then, but he can't. So he gets up, and they talk, and he goes from hand to hand, stares in their eyes, fixes their faces in his memory, as if saying to himself, "He did this? I can't believe it. I am going to kill this one. And this one. . . ."

Those costumes annoyed me. They had too little room around the bottom hem, very narrow. So we walked like we were in 1919 hobble skirts, or Japanese bathrobes. The director wanted this line, nothing sloppy, always vertical and square shapes. Wonderful lines as long as we were standing still. But moving in them . . . they didn't flow. Well, further away, they don't look so bad. But up close like I was . . . I didn't like them.

For most productions of *Julius Caesar,* a "stage knife," a

Figure 61. "O Antony, beg not your death of us." Brutus (Philip Kerr) speaks across Wyman Pendleton as the dead Caesar to the Mark Antony of Michael Levin. Behind them are Metellus Cimber (Theodore Sorel), Cinna (Phillip Taylor), Casca (Rex Everhart), Decius Brutus (Alvah Stanley), and, behind Levin, Trebonius (Larry Carpenter), Act III, scene 1, American Shakespeare Festival, 1973. (Photo, Martha Swope.)

Figure 62. "Let each man render me his bloody hand." Brutus and Mark Antony shake hands over the body of Caesar while Cassius (Lee Richardson) looks on and Cinna, Casca, and Trebonius look away. (Photo, Martha Swope.)

Figure 63. "O, pardon me, thou bleeding piece of earth." Michael Levin in the role of Mark Antony, alone with the body of Caesar (Wyman Pendleton). (Photo, Martha Swope.)

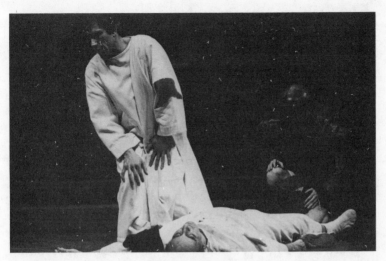

Figure 64. "Passion, I see, is catching." The messenger from Octavius sees the body of Caesar. (Photo, Martha Swope.)

Figure 65. "Thou shalt not back till I have borne this corse / Into the market-place; there I shall try, / In my oration, how the people take / The cruel issue of these bloody men." Michael Levin's Mark Antony makes plans, Act III, scene 1, American Shakespeare Festival, 1973. (Photo, Martha Swope.)

device widely sold in theatrical supply houses, is used in the assassination scene. One can be seen in detail in Figure 37. But another choice was made at the Arena Stage in Washington, D.C., in 1974, and that, as Robert Prosky in the title role there points out, made the scene more difficult to do, especially on that stage with the audience on all four sides of the action.

Robert Prosky on Figure 66:
In the assassination we used short swords, but that made it difficult. It works with a stage knife that collapses into the handle, but a short sword can't do that. And they are dangerous things. I had on a huge leather corset under my robes, and I'm not small to begin with, so this made me look like a hippo. There were blood bags attached to it. Each short sword was built so it would shoot blood down a narrow tube in the blade and onto me. But they leaked! There were a million problems like that, very complicated. They really had to hit me with those swords in this arena theatre. They couldn't just fake it.

I gave the speech about the north star there on those steps. Up behind those steps out of the picture was the flight of stairs down which I had made that triumphal entry earlier in the play. Then here for the assassination, I stayed in one place. The first thrust came from Casca, right in the neck, from behind, then there were a number of others, and then Brutus came very quickly after that. I did not play it as passive, but once Caesar saw that this was Brutus' thrust, then it was like "Give it to me," and that's a better choice than fighting back. Somehow fighting it was too small an action for Caesar.

Lying there all that time after it was over was a problem for me. If the cloth had not been dropped over me in the right way, and if I was in an uncomfortable position, because of that leather corset—it ran from the back of my neck all the way down to my thighs—if that didn't sit right, and if I fell dead in an awkward way, the strap would catch me, here, right back of the neck. Made fifteen minutes seem like forever!

The photographs of the assassination scene at the Arena Stage suggested to Richard Bauer, who played Cassius there in 1974, some of the ways in which the action had to be organized differently from the way it would be on a proscenium stage. Like David Regal, in connection with Figure 11, who played Casca at the Hilberry Classic Theatre in 1968, and Prosky in his interpretation of Caesar in connection with Figure 2, and Jones as Brutus in connection with Figures 59 and 60, Bauer is led by the photograph to discuss his interpretation of Cassius not only in this scene but in the whole play.

Richard Bauer on Figure 66:

The arena staging does present some difficulties in things like the assassination, and in the crowd scenes. It is hard to fill that stage because it is so big, so that it looks as if it were crowded. And the assassination has to be done much more carefully than on a proscenium stage, because in an arena it is seen from all points.

Richard Bauer on Figure 67:

This is a moment after the assassination when we all raise our swords just before we go out to the market-place. That's our Mark Antony, Anderson, over on the right of the picture. My face doesn't show in this shot.

So many critics take the line, from some of the dialogue early in the play, Caesar's line about a lean and hungry look, to mean that Cassius is the villain, but look at this shot. It is Brutus who has persuaded us all to do this blood-

Figure 66. "Every man away: / Brutus shall lead," suggests Cassius (Richard Bayer) at the rear, after the murder of Caesar (Robert Prosky, lying on the floor, foreground), Act III, scene 1, Arena Stage, 1974. (Photo, Alton Miller.)

Figure 67. The assassins raise their red weapons over their heads just before they go to the market place, leaving Mark Antony (Stanley Anderson, in the dark costume, right) with Caesar's body, Act III, scene 1. (Photo, Alton Miller.)

bath. It was a very tense scene in our production, all the way through. Brutus is right, and that means that Cassius is right, to have killed Caesar. He would have destroyed a republic to make himself a king. But the assassination in our production did not turn out to be like a sacrifice. It's just a butchery, the way we did it here, just what Brutus wanted to avoid. Brutus persuades us; it becomes a blood bath; and then Mark Antony in the next scene persuades the crowd; and they commit a blood bath. How does that make Cassius the villain? At the worst he is a politician who knows how politics work.

Stanley Anderson's reaction to the photographs of the moments after the assassination at the Arena Stage in 1974, in which he played the role of Mark Antony, is to comment on the "subtext" of the role, the interior chemistry of the personality of the character and his probable offstage activity.

Stanley Anderson on Figure 67:
Here's a costume that is interesting because of the idea inherent in it. It's the one worn right after the assassination, a rough burlap thing that would have allowed Mark Antony to sneak out of Rome unnoticed and not recognized as the patrician Antony. There was, however, no textual support for this and therefore no way for an audience to realize that this was his reason for dressing like that. But it is a subtext that gives the actor of Antony the embodiment of a prior decision, an active playable choice. In this case, the choice was that, upon hearing of the assassination, he elected to leave the city in fear of his own life. At some point, however, he changed his mind and returned to confront the assassins—an important offstage decision, an active, aggressive one that allowed me to come onstage loaded with all of that history of action as subtext. That helped activate the entrance into that scene as did the

actor who played Antony's messenger, the one who enters into the scene of the conspirators to ask if it was okay for Antony to talk with them. The actor was quite effective at giving the audience the feeling that the water was being tested and that Antony might very well be right around the corner hearing the entire conversation between the messenger and Brutus. Somehow that actor got all of that across.

I carried a hidden knife under that ragged thing and at the end of the scene, after the conspirators had left, I pulled the knife out in a quick movement and dealt with it throughout the remainder of the scene as a symbol of Antony's ineffectuality and failure to aggressively confront an enemy. We, of course, had wanted to maintain a high tension between myself and the conspirators and the fact that the knife was there helped everyone in the scene. This shot is the big "Hail" that was given by all of the conspirators just before they leave, their swords held over their heads. Sometimes, quite spontaneously, I would join in the salute.

Worth comparing with Ric Hamilton's comments on the way he played this moment in connection with Figure 57 and Michael Levin's in connection with Figures 63, 64, and 65, is Stanley Anderson's brief suggestion of how he played the moment at the Arena Stage in 1974.

Stanley Anderson on Figure 68:
This is the first speech alone with the body, "O bleeding piece of earth," after the conspirators have left. It was quite sincere, the first time that Antony has the privacy to deal with the death. It became an oath, a vow, over the body.

Act III of *Julius Caesar* contains the climactic assassination scene, and then follows it with a scene that has become even

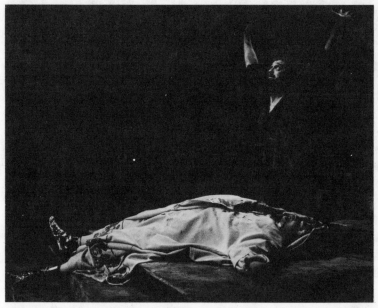

Figure 68. "O, pardon me, thou bleeding piece of earth." Antony, played by Stanley Anderson, alone with the body of Caesar, Act III, scene 1, Arena Stage, 1974. (Photo, Alton Miller.)

more famous in the history of drama, the one containing Mark Antony's funeral oration over the body of Caesar. The very fame of Mark Antony's speech to the citizens in the Forum makes it difficult for an actor, as Ric Hamilton points out in discussing his own performance in the role at Ashland in 1970.

Ric Hamilton on Figures 69 through 74:
In the funeral oration there are a lot of different punctuations in the Folio version from what we get in modern edited versions. I bought a Folio facsimile while I was at Ashland. There are subtle meanings there that seem different. Studying the Folio allowed me to do that speech as if I never heard it before.

One thing I wanted to do was to cover up that first line!

Figure 69. "Be patient till the last." Brutus addresses the citizens from the landing on the stairs, Act III, scene 2, Oregon Shakespearean Festival, 1970. Ric Hamilton as Mark Antony waits his turn to speak lower on the stairs. (Photo, Carolyn Mason-Jones.)

Figure 70. "Friends, Romans, countrymen, lend me your ears." Ric Hamilton as Mark Antony begins his funeral oration on the landing of the stairs, Act III, scene 2, Oregon Shakespearean Festival, 1970. The body of Caesar (Phil Davidson) lies on the bier, front. (Photo, Carolyn Mason-Jones.)

Figure 71. "If you have tears, prepare to shed them now." Mark Antony comes down among the citizens to show them Caesar's wounds. (Photo, Carolyn Mason-Jones.)

Figure 72. ". . . put a tongue / In every wound of Caesar, that should move / The stones . . . to rise and mutiny." Ric Hamilton as Mark Antony incites the crowd. (Photo, Carolyn Mason-Jones.)

Figure 73. ". . . You have forgot the will!" Mark Antony calls the crowd back again. (Photo, Carolyn Mason-Jones.)

Figure 74. "Here is the will." Mark Antony reads the final item in his oration. (Photo, Carolyn Mason-Jones.)

I didn't want everyone in the audience to say, "Oh, yes, I've heard this one before." So I talked the director and the rest of the actors into covering that line up with their speeches and shouts, and quieting down after the speech was started. I started the speech, not at the top of the steps, but, after Brutus had given his, on the way up the stairs, as I was moving to the top.

In my interpretation of the role, Antony was a very loyal person; brilliant; but ruled by emotion. So by the time he got to this funeral oration, he had calmed down enough not to lose control of himself. But he was like a man going into a fight. He knows that he has to win, but he's not exactly sure how he is going to do it. Though he did have some moves up his sleeve. In my own mind, I pretended that Antony had some of his own people, some shills, or a claque, among the members of the mob, ones that he could depend on.

In playing it, I had to keep control of myself, too. My voice tends to rise, to go up in pitch, so it became a problem of keeping the pitch low, to show the relaxation and control that Antony has over himself.

He is both relaxed and calculating. His natural ability had allowed him to get by up to this point without any calculation. The play does divide Antony. At the end of the oration, Antony says, "When comes such another?" and everybody runs off. When we started playing *Julius Caesar* at Ashland, I played what followed as if I were saying to myself, "All right, that's over with; what's next?" as if I were not surprised by what just had happened. By the end of the run of the play, I had begun to exult after they ran off, and sat down on the steps and laughed. I got some flack at first from the director about it, but it felt right. And it pointed up that division within Antony, between the sincere and the scheming man.

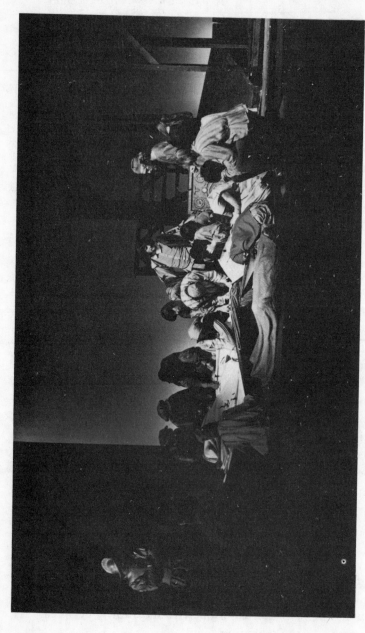

Figure 75. "I . . . / Show you sweet Caesar's wounds, poor poor dumb mouths." Stan Singer as Mark Antony, Act III, scene 2, the funeral oration, University of Kansas, 1973. (Photo, Andrew Tsubaki.)

Stan Singer, who played Mark Antony in the production at Kansas in 1973, describes the blocking of the scene in such a way that it seems to be quite similar to that shown by the photographs of the Ashland production of 1970 in the preceding photographs, though as Figure 75 shows, the Kansas production had a different look from the one at Ashland. Then Singer goes on to comment on the costumes, and on the feeling, so common among actors in this play, that the personality of the character that he is playing is divided.

Stan Singer on Figure 75:
This is the speech over Caesar's body, the funeral oration. The director divided that speech into two parts. In the second part of it, I came down and approached the crowd. Mark Antony showed the people then that he was a part of them. It was blocked with that in mind. At first, then, I was aloof from the crowd, and I spoke to them from one of the levels up above and behind all the figures in this photograph. I spoke in the traditional manner of a Roman orator who addressed a group.

There are certain measured rhythms in the first part of that speech as if the character Antony does not know where he stands. Then after that I gave the speech a steady build in volume, but cautiously, as if Mark Antony knew that the mob was a dangerous entity.

Those togas that we wore were awkward for me there. I had to come down the steps, into the crowd, and there were many nights when I was standing there, giving part of the speech with one of the citizens standing on my hem. I had to yank it out every now and then. That does detract from concentration. I really wondered, sometimes, am I going to be able to get to the next place that I must be standing in order to make sense of the lines coming up? But visually, as you can see from the photographs, those togas were very impressive.

I enjoyed playing with the duality of Antony, the ambiguity of whether he was a good or evil man. For instance, in the funeral speech, I turned my back to the audience a few times and then lowered my head and turned it a little so the audience could see my eyes, turning to check on the onstage mob, to see if the mob was buying what I had to say. The theatre audience caught that. Every interesting character is double. If he is only one-sided, the actor has to give him another side or the audience will lose interest.

In this photograph I have finished the first part of the oration, and I'm down in the crowd, touching as many of them as I can, as if I had to convince them that I was not afraid of them, that I was a part of them.

At the end of this speech, the whole crowd disperses, and I was by myself. I interpreted the character as if it were the first thrill of power and manipulation that Antony had felt. I played it as if I were thrilled with knowing that I could tell a mass of people one thing, and still go behind the scenes and do exactly what I intend to do, for my own ambitions.

Costumes are among the first things William Wright reacts to in the photograph of himself as Mark Antony at Cumston Hall in Maine; he immediately gives a long and detailed description of the action between himself and the actors playing the citizens during his delivery of the funeral oration, pointing out, too, the problems posed for the actor by the familiarity of the speech.

William Wright on Figure 76:
We used authentic Roman costumes in Maine, so while Brutus was giving his oration in the scene of the funeral, I was offstage getting ten square yards of black mourning toga draped about me. That's it in this photograph.

We staged the funeral oration so that we used the au-

Figure 76. "I . . . / Show you sweet Caesar's wounds, poor poor dumb mouths." William Wright as Mark Antony over the body of Caesar (John-Frederick Jones), Act III, scene 2, the funeral oration, Monmouth, Maine, 1973. (Photo, Arthur Griffiths.)

dience as the people of Rome. I played all of the oration directly out front and looked people in the auditorium in the eye. In the meantime, our people, our mobilus, ran up stairs and were in the balcony looking and yelling over the railing from up there. The first line of the speech I separated with pauses. They were shouting all the time. An audience, when it hears the beginning of a famous speech, like "Friends, Romans, countrymen, lend me your ears," they just sit back and relax, as if they were getting into a warm tub! So we tried to take the onus off that by obscuring the first three words, even the next line, so the mobilus up in the balcony yelled all the time during those first two lines, to drown them out, and by then I'd be into the speech and the audience would listen to it.

Antony in that speech has his plans, but he is winging it, or that's the way I played it, he is winging it only insofar as a debater wings it. Antony is there to rebut Brutus. He's of the Roman class that is trained in rhetoric. He can speak extemporaneously, to move the mobilus. Only in that regard is he winging it. But I don't show that in acting it any more than any actor shows himself to be speaking off the top of his head, because that is what acting is, looking as if one were making up the words as he goes along.

As the mobilus in the balcony got more and more aroused, they began to respond to me by yelling, and I had to stop now and then. Then as it began to build momentum, they began to be moved. They finally rushed down the stairs in the back of the auditorium, up the orchestra aisles, leapt onto the stage, caught up the body of Caesar and bore him off.

Wyman Pendleton is probably the only actor among those interviewed for this book who had actually seen the famous production of *Julius Caesar* staged by Orson Welles. In fact, he acted a small part in it, one that he recalls when com-

Figure 77. Michael Levin as Mark Antony in the funeral oration, Act III, scene 2, American Shakespeare Festival, 1973. Caesar (Wyman Pendleton) is on the bier, visible behind Levin. (Photo, Martha Swope.)

menting on the funeral oration in the production at the American Shakespeare Festival in Connecticut in 1973.

Wyman Pendleton on Figure 77:
I am there just behind Michael Levin as Mark Antony, on the bier, during the funeral oration. Yes, I played the corpse myself. No problem until he strips the cover away to show the body.

When I went to Brown University in 19 . . . well, we won't go into the year . . . when Orson Welles was doing his famous modern-dress Caesar, the road company for that production started out in Providence. I was in that road production there as one of the citizens. Went to Boston with it too. It was all done as a Hitleresque thing. They had a coffin, but neither a dummy nor their Caesar in it. They had an extra in it. That's all he did, just lie in that box! Just in case, on the road, they played in theatres that had balconies from which some members of the audience could see into the box!

Michael Levin describes how as Mark Antony in the American Shakespeare Festival production of *Julius Caesar* in 1973, he played the speech of the funeral oration. Note the similarity between his ideas and those suggested by Ric Hamilton for his performance at Ashland in 1970.

Michael Levin on Figure 77:
In our production they made the plebes, the mob, very important in the funeral oration, lots of expressive movement. It was a big production; we had twenty extras on stage. The director found that the crowd was an excellent tool for this sort of expression through more than just vocal means, and he made them a real force in the play. But in this photograph it shows how Antony gets the focus anyway. It's a classic speech and it works like dynamite. Of course, I had to shut the citizens up at the beginning, a little bit at a time.

There was an enormous build to that speech. He isn't all that nasty at first on Brutus and Cassius and the honorable men. He dissembles. But then he gets the crowd hooked on how much they loved Caesar. And as they respond, he feeds on them, and the more they love him, the more they love Caesar, the further he goes, until it's out of control. He doesn't know what's going to happen next, but he lets it go. He goes all out. At the end he really dissembles with the will. I played him as stunned when they rioted at the end, as he might say to himself, "Wow, I did it!" He's on a cloud.

The budget controls the number of extras who can be hired and costumed. Michael Levin pointed out that the production at the American Shakespeare Festival in 1973 was big; it had twenty extras. Some differences in staging problems then become evident. Twenty seemed a lot on that huge stage in Stratford, Connecticut, but at the Arena Stage in Washington, D.C., as Richard Bauer, who played Cassius there, points out, twenty people in the crowd did not seem enough.

Richard Bauer on Figure 78:
We had only twenty extras, and on a proscenium stage, that would be a lot, but we could have used fifty; more would have been even better. If you disperse twenty people around on the stage at the Arena, they look like a small group, like this one here, as our Brutus gives his speech in the Forum after the assassination, and just before Mark Antony gives his. In a proscenium staging a director can fill up the two edges of the stage with extras, or range them along the front of the apron so that the audience becomes a part of the crowd. But this is much more difficult in an arena. Twenty is not enough and even twenty is expensive for costumes, salaries, and so forth. Fifty or hundred is mind-boggling. Shakespeare had the same problem, but he didn't have an arena stage to fill up.

Like Denny Lipscomb at the Hilberry Classic Theatre in 1968, Gary Bayer played the role of Octavius Caesar, a character who never comes onstage until Act IV. Therefore, like Lipscomb in Figures 1 and 84, Bayer played a member

Figure 78. "Be patient till the last." Brutus (James Blendick) gives the first oration in the market-place, Act III, scene 2, Arena Stage, 1974. (Photo, Alton Miller.)

of the crowd of citizens in earlier scenes to help fill the stage. He comments that some of the effects shown in the photograph are not the same as those of the actual performances.

Gary Bayer on Figures 79 and 80:
I was one of the population again here in the funeral oration. The photographs of it here are more brightly lit than it was in the actual performance. In performance it was largely lit by torchlight, and that lent itself to this big space in this play.

Stanley Anderson as Mark Antony at the Arena Stage also points out that the photographs taken during rehearsals, do not exactly reflect the play as it was subsequently performed on opening night and afterward; then he too, like Bauer in connection with Figure 78, comments on the problem of creating a convincing crowd onstage.

Stanley Anderson on Figures 79 and 80:
During the course of rehearsal, our whole concept for the character of Antony underwent some changes. We began with him as the consummate politician who would do anything—in fact, did all sorts of things—to gain his own ends. By the opening night much of that had changed, though we never did see him as quite the heroic figure that I understand he has been interpreted as in other productions.

For instance, in these shots of the funeral oration, we began with my showing a robe that was clearly not the one that Caesar wore into the Senate, but a robe that Antony had in fact torn, put blood on. But there was no way that an audience would understand that it was Antony who made the switch, and not some sloppy properties manager offstage. There was just no text to support it. And finally we got rid of it, after these photographs were taken.

Figure 79. "If you have tears, prepare to shed them now." Mark Antony, played by Stanley Anderson, in the funeral oration Act III, scene 2, Arena Stage, 1974. (Photo, Alton Miller.)

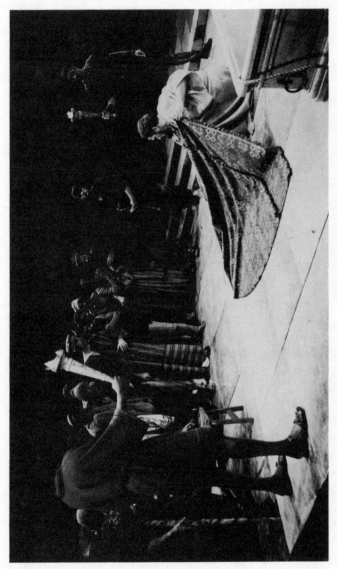

Figure 80. "You all do know this mantle." Mark Antony with the cloak of Caesar, Act III, scene 2, Arena Stage, 1974. (Photo, Alton Miller.)

I began the funeral oration having to shut the crowd up gradually. We didn't have an enormous crowd, and in this arena, we·needed one. We tried at first to stylize the crowd and have it at the center, as this photograph shows. But the size of what Antony has to say simply didn't match the size of that little group. So before the end of rehearsals, but again, after these photographs were taken, we moved the crowd out to the fringes of the stage, so that the audience became a part of the crowd. Of course, I still played with the crowd. There were moments when I paused, not only to regain my breath, but also to listen to what members of the crowd were saying, to hear how they were taking my speech.

Wyman Pendleton noted in connection with Figure 77 that ·he played the corpse himself on the big stage at Stratford, Connecticut. It is clear that Jones plays the corpse himself in Figure 76 of the production in Monmouth, Maine. And the actor of Caesar at Ashland also plays the corpse himself, as is evident in Figures 70-74. But at the Arena Stage in 1974, even though they had the corpse in a casket that only partially concealed it from the audience, they did not use Robert Prosky, the actor of Caesar, as the corpse, but built a substitute.

Robert Prosky on Figures 81 and 82:
The corpse there is a fake. They made a very good one here in the shop at the Arena Stage. I had to make it up every night at the same time as I put on my own make-up, so we'd both look alike. After the run of the play, they had a fund-raising auction of old props here at the Arena, and they sold the dummy along with that lot. My kids wanted me to put in a bid on it, but somehow . . . I didn't really want it around the house . . .

Figure 81. "I tell you that which you yourselves do know." Mark Antony prepares to shock the crowd in the market-place, Act III, scene 2, Arena Stage, 1974. (Photo, Alton Miller.)

Figure 82. "I . . . / Show you sweet Caesar's wounds, poor poor dumb mouths." Mark Antony displays the corpse of Caesar, Act III scene 2, Arena Stage, 1974. (Photo, Alton Miller.)

Figure 83. "Here was a Caesar! When comes such another?" Mark Antony, played by Stanley Anderson, finishes his oration and the reading of the will, Act III, scene 2, Arena Stage, 1974. (Photo, Alton Miller.)

Reminiscent of Hamilton's comment on the end of the funeral oration at Ashland in 1970 in connection with Figure 74 is Stanley Anderson's comment on the same moment in the Arena Stage production in 1974.

Stanley Anderson on Figure 83:
At the end, after the crowd had all run off to get the conspirators, my last speech alone on stage there had a cry of victory in it.

Richard Spear, who directed the production of *Julius Caesar* at the Hilberry Classic Theatre in 1968, briefly points out that, like the Arena Stage in 1974, as pictured in Figures 81 and 82, he used a dummy for the corpse, and that he too had problems generating enough people to create the effect

Figure 84. "I . . . / Show you sweet Caesar's wounds, poor poor dumb mouths." Mark Antony (Earl D. A. Smith), center, in the funeral oration, Act III, scene 2, Hilberry Classic Theatre, 1968. Denny Lipscomb, later to play Octavius, kneels left at the feet of the body. David Regal, who earlier played Casca, stands in the orchestra pit to the right of the head of the body. (Photo, Wayne State University Photo Services.)

of a crowd. He then goes on, like Wright in connection with Figure 76, to describe the blocking of the scene at the Hilberry.

Richard Spear on Figure 84:
We tried to do the funeral oration including the whole room. We never have enough actors to make it seem that there is a mob. But it worked very well. I always thought that the body would get a laugh when we uncovered it. But it didn't. Apparently it was grim enough that it per-suaded people that it wasn't funny. The grouping here was started on the ramps around the back of the auditorium at the beginning of the speech. Antony calls them forward and gradually moved them in while we localized the light as we got near the end of the scene, until the only light focused on Antony and the body. Then suddenly they dispersed, all of them—action!—as they went out to loot, to burn . . .

David Regal played Casca at the Hilberry Classic Theatre in 1968, and though Casca is not ostensibly killed by the mob until after this scene is over, he disappears from the play at the end of the previous scene; so Regal was enlisted to help fill the stage as part of the mob in this scene.

David Regal on Figure 84:
Here I am down front in the funeral oration. I am not Casca anymore in this one. Everybody who had died had to come to help fill up the crowd .We came down the aisle, we were in the audience, all over the whole theatre. We had some problems I remember with our responses to Mark Antony's speech. Sometimes there wasn't enough. Other times some guy would get so into it that he'd come out with, "You got it!" or "You're exactly right!" which jarred, because it wasn't in iambic pentameter!

Denny Lipscomb, like Gary Bayer at the Arena Stage in 1974, played Octavius Caesar at the Hilberry Classic Theatre in 1968, and since Octavius does not appear until Act IV, Lipscomb spent the first three acts of the production playing a member of the crowds.

Denny Lipscomb on Figure 84:
Here's the funeral oration. I was still playing a member of the populace here right there by the body, kneeling near its feet. I had only a few seconds, or so it seemed, before the end of this scene and the beginning of the next one, to get my gold armor on in order to begin playing Octavius.

Julius Caesar:
Act IV

Denny Lipscomb's reaction to Figure 85, which shows him as Octavius Caesar in the production by the Hilberry Classic Theatre, is marked to some extent by his realization that he was much younger and less experienced when he played the role in 1968, as his final remarks reveal, but even so these comments also show the kind of careful analysis of character that actors go through, even for a small part.

Denny Lipscomb on Figure 85:
What I was trying to do was to show the arrogance of this young and obnoxious person. Because his name is Caesar, he thinks that he's merely going to use Antony as is necessary, then get rid of him. There is one other little scene later in the play, just before the battle, in which Antony and Octavius disagree about who is going to put his army where, and as I say, "I do not cross you, but I will do so," I gave him a look that implied that as soon as we had won the battle, I was going to see that he got his. I saw Octavius in that play as a Caligula. To show you how young I was then, I was rehearsing it like that at the beginning, almost with a German accent! Silly, but that was the idea, arrogance and superiority complex. Very mental. Antony gets caught up in all those emotional things, but Octavius is not the one who feels. I played about all the opportunities I had to show that, but they weren't many. It's a small part.

As Lipscomb points out, the play contrasts Antony and Octavius, and Richard Bauer, who played Cassius at the Arena Stage in 1974, points out that in the subsequent scene,

119

Figure 85. "He shall not live. Look, with a spot I damn him." The triumvirate meets in Act IV, scene 1, Hilberry Classic Theatre, 1968. Left to right are a servant (Jim Newell), Mark Antony (Earl D. A. Smith), Octavius played by Denny Lipscomb, and Lepidus (George Spelvin). (Photo, Wayne State University Photo Services.)

Figure 86. "You wrong me in every way; you wrong me, Brutus." Richard Bauer as Cassius and Brutus (James Blendick) in the "tent scene," Act IV, scene 3, Arena Stage, 1974. (Photo Alton Miller.)

one that actors all call the "tent scene," Brutus a
are contrasted in a similar way.

Richard Bauer on Figure 86:
In the tent scene we have a falling out between Cassius and
Brutus—Cassius the good military technician and Brutus
who is not. Cassius has just pulled an acceptable political
trick, which the flaming liberal, Brutus, is against. One of
the best scenes in the play! Works like gangbusters! Two
men resolve their differences in a very open way, ugly
words, lots of hurt and emotion. Then they get more and
more bad news. And once again, Cassius defers to Brutus.
Brutus makes grave errors; Cassius warns him, but he
keeps on deferring to Brutus. That tent scene is the key to
the character of Cassius. The danger is that Cassius can
become the incredible villain in the first half. Then in
the second half he's not any more. How do you rectify
the two? Well, Cassius never is a villain. That Cassius is
a villain is bad scholarship, the stuff that the audience
brings to the theatre in their heads. The actor has to fight
that. I don't know if it is possible for an actor to defeat it.
He is ultra-conservative, a practiced politician. But the
tent scene is affecting. We embraced and wept together.
Then Cassius finds out that Portia is dead, and then they
prepare for a battle that Cassius knows is a mistake.

Like Bauer, Richard Greene sees a contrast in character
between Brutus and Cassius. When Greene played Cassius
at the Hilberry Classic Theatre in 1968, the difference was
underlined by a contrast between his acting style and that of
the man playing Brutus. He begins his comments by describing the blocking of the tent scene and then comments on the
costumes.

Richard Greene on Figures 87 and 88:
This is the tent scene at the Hilberry. A pole and canvas

Figure 87. "You wrong me in every way; you wrong me, Brutus." Brutus (E. Lee Smith) listens grudgingly to Cassius, played by Richard Greene, in the tent scene, Act IV, scene 3, Hilberry Classic Theatre, 1968. (Photo, Wayne State University Photo Service.)

Figure 88. "Now sit we close . . . / And call in question our necessities." Brutus at center welcomes Titinius and Messala and other soldiers while Cassius looks on from lower left and the servant Lucius from upper left, Act IV, scene 3, Hilberry Classic Theatre, 1968. (Photo, Wayne State University Photo Services.)

structure upstage left suggested the entrance. To begin with, the scene demands privacy. The door must be closed, the rest of the world shut out. When we issued the order to leave us, the soldiers lowered the large tent flap and went to sentinel positions off left. It's remarkable how such a simple gesture, supported by a slight adjustment of the lights, can so transform a stage. In one military movement, the atmosphere went from public to private.

I liked this battle costume. It was heavy and leather and had a sense of full harness. You feel invincible in that kind of gear.

As actors, the man playing Brutus and I worked with dissimilar technique. It led us, ironically, into a very healthy antagonism. It fed the scene, one of the finest one-on-one confrontations in all Shakespeare.

The tent scene receives a different emphasis from the point of view of an actor playing Brutus. But John-Frederick Jones, who played the role in the production of 1976 at the Old Globe Theatre in Los Angeles, suggests as well the contrast between Cassius and Brutus.

John-Frederick Jones on Figure 89:
In a play like this, one guide to finding a character or a way to move onstage is to look for opposites. If Brutus is still, Cassius moves. If Cassius is still, Brutus is energized. Shakespeare has the stoic Octavius and the epicurean Mark Antony mirrored in Brutus and Cassius. The scene in the tent in Act IV is like a teeter-totter. Cassius, when he enters, is full-blown; Brutus is quiet, preoccupied. He does not want to let personal matters interfere with the business of the state. He already knows that Portia is dead but he hasn't told anyone about it. Then Brutus gets angry at Cassius. It's quite often the scene in a production in which those two actors earn their money. We see Brutus at the end of his tether. No fight left in him. I don't

Figure 89. "Now sit we close . . . / And call in question our necessities." Brutus, played by John-Frederick Jones, with the two soldiers and Cassius (Frank Savino) in the tent scene, Act IV, scene 3, Old Globe Theatre, Los Angeles, 1976. (Photo, Mitchell Rose.)

really think the scene ought to be a shouting match. Cassius certainly has to be angry and hot-blooded, and right off the top of his head, but Brutus is not. He gets angry, but not screaming angry. It's the anger of a man who sees the end.

Brutus' action throughout the tent scene is to continue the business of winning battles. He doesn't want to talk about personal injury, the way Cassius does. He doesn't want to talk about Portia, which, when they find out about her, is what Cassius and the other characters want to talk about. One of the others had a piece of paper with the news. He wants to offer condolences, but Brutus doesn't want to talk about it. He goes back to maps on this desk here, as if to say, "Let's talk about this."

These are the two commanders who come in. This is the moment when Brutus says, "Farewell Portia." In front of the men he doesn't break down. He comforts other people rather than be comforted himself. "Then what do you think of marching to Philippi?" He's back to work. They all feel sorry for him and he's looking at them, saying to himself, "I've got to bring them back to the matter at hand." So we made in Los Angeles a moment of this. Some academics say that it looks a little cheap if Brutus is going to use Portia's death merely as a demonstration of his stoicism. I don't think it's cheap. It helps the others handle it. Cassius, on the right, is in the midst of saying, "I have so much as this in art as you, yet my nature . . . " —that is, if it had been me, I would have broken down. The point to the scene is that Brutus wants to get back to the work at hand. The fact that he's drawn away from it is what makes the scene live. The audience can see his movements saying, "I don't want to talk about that, but this."

Similar to Jones' analysis of the scene is that of another

Figure 90. "Now sit we close . . . / And call in question our necessities." William Kuhlke, as Brutus, standing center, with soldiers in the tent scene, Act IV, scene 3, University of Kansas, 1973. (Photo, Andrew Tsubaki.)

Figure 91. "Is not the leaf turned down / Where I left reading?" Lucius falls asleep, and Brutus, played by William Kuhlke, is about to take up a book just as the ghost of Caesar (David Cook) appears, in the tent scene, Act IV, scene 3, University of Kansas, 1973. (Photo, Andrew Tsubaki.)

actor in the role of Brutus, William Kuhlke, who played it at the University of Kansas in 1973. Kuhlke is reacting against published critical comments, ones that Jones had in mind as well, that Brutus can be made to look a bit pompous during the moments when he shows off his stoicism at the news of his wife's death, news that he had already heard before the messenger arrived. Kuhlke does not want to allow the chance that Brutus will seem pompous to arise.

William Kuhlke on Figure 90:
Here Brutus chooses to present a lesson to his troops, before Philippi, in the way he receives, for the second time, the news of his wife's death. It was our interpretation that he does that purposely in order to provide for his troops a stoic lesson about the way to comfort oneself in the face of catastrophe, which he hopes they will carry onto the battlefield.

In Figure 91 Kuhlke at Kansas in 1973 is pictured at the moment when the ghost of Caesar appears, just before it speaks to him in the tent scene. Wyman Pendleton, who played Caesar at the American Shakespeare Festival in Stratford, Connecticut, describes how it felt to play the ghost and goes on to describe audience reactions to the tent scene.

Wyman Pendleton on Figure 92:
We played eight or ten weeks of school audiences with this production. The scene in the tent with Brutus and Cassisu got them down. Everything else was clear for them, but that tent scene, though it's good talk, just got them down. They would love it when I'd appear as the ghost. A lot depends, of course, on how well-prepared the kids have been by their teachers. If they come knowing what to expect, the scene goes well. But unlike the adult audiences, they like the battle scenes in the last act. Adults liked the tent scene!

Figure 92. "Is not the leaf turned down / Where I left reading?" Brutus (Philip Kerr) at his book just as the ghost of Caesar, played by Wyman Pendleton, appears, in the tent scene, Act IV, scene 3, American Shakespeare Festival, 1973. (Photo, Martha Swope.)

As the ghost in this photograph, I was up a ladder, in back of a sheet of scrim, a cheesecloth-like screen that only shows something if there's a light behind the screen on the thing. That's me there over Brutus' head, way up in the air. I never saw it, myself, of course, so I cannot say much more about it than this photograph shows.

This same scene as that shown in Figures 91 and 92, at Kansas and in Connecticut, respectively, produced an inventive moment for Earl McCarroll in Maine at the 1973 production, which he directed.

Earl McCarroll:
An exciting thing happened in rehearsal when we were doing the tent scene. The ghost of Caesar, John-Frederick Jones, was speaking. Then after the ghost leaves, Brutus wakes up the sleeping Lucius and says, "Why did you cry out?" And I suddenly thought, "I've been missing it! Lucius is the medium, obviously, for the ghost! The ghost can't speak!" So we staged it that way, with the words of the ghost coming out of the mouth of the sleeping Lucius. I don't know if it has been done that way before, but it seemed completely right to me and completely new. And it's right there in the lines!

Julius Caesar:
Act V

The battle scenes of the last act of *Julius Caesar* are sometimes photogenic, but actors seldom have much to say about the photographs of those scenes. Raye Birk, who played Cassius at the Oregon Shakespearean Festival at Ashland in 1970, is moved by such photographs to suggest that this part of the play is a kind of anticlimax and then to link it to an earlier quiet scene, the tent scene.

Raye Birk on Figure 93:
It was hard to do *Julius Caesar* well. We all found some solace in the fact that no one had heard of many successful productions. Oh, there was Orson Welles' thing, but we all thought that it was based on a gimmick. In the tragedies it is Act IV that breaks your back. Modern audiences are not used to a lengthy quiet period before the big climactic scene. The tent scene, between Brutus and I, was one of my favorites, but the audience was ho-humming by that time, and the audiences at Ashland are some of the most supportive that an actor will ever play to. These photographs are after the tent scene. This is the quarrel first between Antony and Octavius, and then the quarrel among the four of us, Antony and Octavius against Brutus and myself.

Photographs of the same scene in the same production at Ashland also provoke from Ric Hamilton, who played the role of Mark Antony, first a reflection back to the beginning of Act IV, the earlier scene between Octavius and Antony (compare the Hilberry production, Figure 85) and then to the end of the play (compare the productions at Kansas,

133

Figure 93. "I do not cross you, but I will do so." Octavius Caesar (J. Steven White) with soldiers, center, in a brief disagreement with Ric Hamilton as Mark Antony, right, Act V, scene 1, Oregon Shakespearean Festival, 1970. (Photo, Carolyn Mason-Jones.)

Figure 94. "Antony, / The posture of your blows are yet unknown." Ric Hamilton as Mark Antony, left and Brutus (Tom Donaldson) hear Raye Birk as Cassius speak, Act V, scene 1, Oregon Shakespearean Festival, 1970. (Photo, Carolyn Mason-Jones.)

Figure 95. "A peevish school-boy . . . / Join'd with a masker and a reveller!" From left, Octavius and Mark Antony (Ric Hamilton) prepare to go back to their troops, watched by Brutus and followed by insults from Cassius (Raye Birk), Act V, scene 1, Oregon Shakespearean Festival, 1970. (Photo, Carolyn Mason-Jones.)

at the Stratford Festival in Connecticut, and at the Arena Stage, Figures 99, 100, and 101), the last speech that Mark Antony has over the body of Brutus.

Ric Hamilton on Figures 94 and 95:
This is the scene before the battle, a typical Shakespeare bow-wow scene like in a history play, warriors blustering at each other. The scene is a sequel to that earlier one with Lepidus, the triumvirate scene, where they made up that blacklist. The actor doing Octavius played him as very cold. Antony was flushed with success and confident, and he didn't want to be devious. That scene summed him up with his line, "So is my horse," as if there were no great obstacle that could not be handled, a great confidence in

Figure 96. "Defiance, traitors, hurl we in your teeth." Stan Singer as Mark Antony, left, with drawn sword, watches Octavius (Rodger M. Smith) climb the barricade. On the platform are William Kuhlke in the role of Brutus, with Cassius (Fred Vesper), Act V, scene 1. University of Kansas, 1973. (Photo, Andrew Tsubaki.)

Antony. That was the beginning of the end for him. He declines from there on.

By the time that *Julius Caesar* is over, Octavius is ascending and Antony's period of power is really over. His last speech in the play over the body of Brutus is a heartfelt speech. He is reacting to the world emotionally again, rather than analytically, and that's his later undoing.

Stan Singer discusses the photograph of the same moment in the production of *Julius Caesar* at Kansas in 1973, in which he played Mark Antony, describing how the scene was blocked.

Stan Singer on Figure 96:

Yes, the challenge before the battle. We shouted across this gap. Brutus and Cassius are up on that high platform. We had taken some of these stands and turned them upside down or on their sides, as if they were barricades. That makes a very compressed battlefield, obviously. Octavius and I are down here with these guards in back of us. We are yelling back and forth. This is the scene in which Octavius shows his leadership over Mark Antony. They first have the quarrel that echoes the tent scene between Brutus and Cassius, and it is Octavius who changes the plan, who won't take his army this way but that. The audience gets the idea when Octavius says he won't contest Mark Antony *now;* that later on there will be a falling out. The director blocked it so that I stood back and Octavius took the forefront, even crawled up on the barricade, waved his fist. I made my comments from back here. Octavius' lines are to the effect that he wanted the fight to start right here, and my lines are saying, in effect, "We know what sneaks you guys are. . . ." That's an interesting little element there, the contrast between Mark Antony and Octavius. Opposite them it is Brutus who is standing forward and Cassius who is hanging back.

Figure 97. "Defiance hurl we in your teeth." Stanley Anderson as Mark Antony (left rear) and Gary Bayer as Octavius (rear center) shout at Brutus, Cassius, and their officers in the foreground just before the battle, Act V, scene 1, Arena Stage, 1974. (Photo, Alton Miller.)

Gary Bayer, speaking of the same scene at the Arena Stage in 1974, where he played the role of Octavius Caesar, links it to the earlier scene with Lepidus (see Figure 85), and as a contrasting conflict to the quarrel between Brutus and Cassius in the earlier tent scene (see Figure 86). He also speaks of the way it was blocked at the Arena acting area.

Gary Bayer on Figure 97:
That's a tricky thing when they meet on the field before the battle, Octavius and Antony on one side, Cassius and Brutus on the other, all square off. It was tricky even given the space we had. We were hurling insults at each other as if from one hill to the next, as if there were a little creek between the hills. Easier for us on the Arena Stage than on a proscenium stage, but still that problem existed. We had to project, really yell, yet at the same time, it was obvious to the audience how really close we are. At the same time, he had that conflict between Octavius and Antony going on, beginning to brew, and it's obvious that Octavius joining Antony was a purely political act and in the mind of Octavius, to be very short-lived. No questions of loyalty are involved.

The tent scene between Brutus and Cassius was being played very emotionally, so Anderson, the actor of Mark Antony, and I tried for something different, totally calculated. Octavius is methodically squeezing Antony out, establishing himself, every chance he gets. He makes it known with a word or two that he is in charge. The seeds had been started in that earlier scene with Lepidus, making the blacklist. Octavius' gifts are not oratory or personality; he's a manager. That's what I worked for in that scene with Lepidus.

But in that battlefield face-off, I always felt pressed for

space. I wished that there were more. The two camps were too close . . . and then we could have got more mileage out of the little personal conflict between Antony and Octavius. I tended to talk a line in that scene, back and forth, to the tree and back, when I attempt to assert myself, metronoming it off, back and fourth.

Stanley Anderson, on the other hand, playing Mark Antony in that same scene at the Arena Stage, links the scene to the speech he gives later over the body of Brutus (see Figure 101) during the last moments of the play.

Stanley Anderson on Figure 97:
In the challenge scene before the battle, we worked on the diagonal across the arena space, standing one group in the mouth of one corner and the opposing group in the opposing corner. Although Antony in the text is shunted to the rear in favor of Octavius after the oration, I never felt driven from the focus by the Octavius of Gary Bayer. It is after all, to an Antony's advantage to give his Octavius more worth than is hinted in the text, to make him a worthy adversary. Antony would have liked to be in Octavius' position, and my reactions to observing what Octavius is, his rigidity, his manner of dealing with people, his opinions on action and the future, gave spark to the burst that comes at the end over Brutus' body, when Octavius has failed to give even the warrior his due honor, not acknowledging Brutus as a soldier or a misguided human. It allows Antony to see his own prospects under an Octavius.

John-Frederick Jones, reacting to a photograph of himself as Brutus standing over the corpse of Cassius, gives an account of his own analysis of the kind of internal conflict he wishes to project as Brutus. He played the role in the 1976 production at the Old Globe Theatre in Los Angeles.

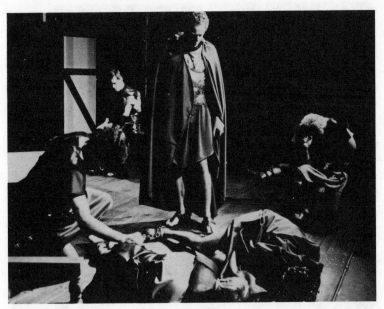

Figure 98. "I owe more tears / To this dead man than you shall see me pay." John-Frederick Jones as Brutus finds the body of Cassius, Act V, scene 3, Old Globe Theatre, Los Angeles, 1976. (Photo, Mitchell Rose.)

John-Frederick Jones on Figure 98:
Cassius' death begins to enlarge and increase the burden of responsibilities for Brutus. You see, he feels responsible for Caesar's death, Portia's death, and now Cassius. The burden is very heavy—but he doesn't break. The play is tightening its focus, it's becoming the tragedy of Brutus. This is a very tender, touching moment over the corpse, but the actor must resist breaking down. "I owe more tears / To this dead man than you shall see me pay." It may seem a little cruel, and the director may feel you are missing a moment of sympathy, but remember Brutus is a stoic; it's not that he doesn't feel but that he must not let his feeling rule.

Figure 99. "This was the noblest Roman of them all." Stan Singer as Mark Antony, center, holding helmet, delivers a funeral oration over the body of Brutus, Act V, scene 5, University of Kansas, 1973. (Photo, Andrew Tsubaki.)

Technically, his final moment is just ahead, and he must sustain tension, keep the wheel turned tight but not release the momentum.

When Brutus finally breaks, it is for everything and everyone but himself. He is kind and thoughtful to his men, even to the last. "My heart doth joy that yet in all my life / I found no man but he was true to me." Remember Brutus is truly noble. He always thinks of the other, and never considers self—ever. That is a Roman.

In a pattern similar to that displayed by Jones as Brutus, Stan Singer, who was Mark Antony in the production at the University of Kansas in 1973, gives an analysis of the internal conflicts of that character as a reaction to this photograph of himself giving his last speech over the body of Brutus.

Stan Singer on Figure 99:
Antony doesn't really know what he's gotten himself into. That speech when he talks over Brutus' body at the end I found was significant because we finally get the idea that Antony would have taken a different path from this one if he had had the chance to take it, and here he regrets the fact that not only is Caesar dead, but also Brutus. And Brutus, he realizes here, is a better man than he can be.

Wyman Pendleton played Caesar at the American Shakespeare Festival in Stratford, Connecticut, in 1973, and therefore he does not appear in the last act of the play at all, so his reaction to this photograph of the last moment in that production is to comment on the costumes.

Wyman Pendleton on Figure 100:
All the togas were fine, but the people who had to wear the armor were in misery. It was all leather, all articulated,

Figure 100. "This was the noblest Roman of them all." Michael Levin as Mark Antony, left, delivers a funeral oration over the body of Brutus (Philip Kerr), center, while sharing the stage with Octavius (Richard Backus), right, Act V, scene 5, American Shakespeare Festival, 1973. (Photo, Martha Swope.)

but still. . . . One reason they used such big armor, of course, was that they had such a big stage to fill. You need size even to walk out on that stage. All the leading characters worked to get their helmets off as soon as possible, carried them at the hip, or like in this photograph. That helmet, they said, did funny things to the voice. They couldn't tell what you were doing with all those ear flaps over the head. Fortunately for me, Caesar wore a black leather wreath, so there was no worry about that on my part.

Michael Levin played Mark Antony in the same production with Pendleton. His comments here on costumes make an interesting comparison with those he makes in reference to Figures 61 through 65, and with Richard Greene's comments in reference to Figures 87 and 88. Levin then describes the effect of the scene that the production sought to achieve.

Michael Levin on Figure 100:
Oh, those warrior costumes. Like big beetles. I never liked the helmet. Of course, the size of the house and that big stage had a lot to do with the design of the warrior costumes. That is a huge place.

In this final scene I had equal focus with Octavius. Oh, I took the focus on the speech over the body of Brutus, but then as in this photograph here, we had an equal footing which, of course, indicates that Octavius is on the rise and the force to be reckoned with in the future. That's the image that ended the play.

Gary Bayer, Octavius at the Arena Stage in 1974, describes the last effect sought for in that production in terms reminiscent of those suggested by Anderson, the Mark Antony in the same production.

Figure 101. "This was the noblest Roman of them all." Stanley Anderson as Mark Antony, left, delivers a funeral oration over the body of Brutus, while Octavius, played by Gary Bayer, far right, listens, Act V, scene 5, Arena Stage, 1974. (Photo, Alton Miller.)

Gary Bayer on Figure 101:
This scene is the end of the play. There is a put-down of
Mark Antony in this moment. He has this speech about
Brutus, has the focus, but down here, not up on that
little hill with Octavius. My movements toward him were
abrupt, as if to say, "Get it over with," or "Come on, let's
go." By this time Octavius is ignoring Antony. Octavius
knows that this has to be said about Brutus. Public re-
lations require it. Since Antony can say it better, Octavius has him say it, and waits for him to get it over with,
as if it were not even a point of conflict because the speech
was only trappings, decoration.

Suggestions for Writing Assignments

Actors naturally speak not so much of the meaning of the whole play as of their own roles within it. Even so, the concepts of these seven productions of *Julius Caesar* seem clear enough, and quite similar. Most of them are conservative, attempting simply to "tell the story" in a straightforward way. Yet even within those limits there are some variations— variations that are interesting to explore.

One place to start is with the photographs. A comparison and contrast of the settings and styles of costumes is one kind of study. A more subtle and difficult, but often rewarding, study is that of "blocking," the way the actors and groups of actors have been directed to place themselves on the different stages and the way the blocking is connected to the size and shape of the stage and auditorium.

The size of the stage is also reflected in many of the actors' comments on these photographs, and another good, brief essay could be developed simply on the various ways the actors have described what their stages were like. Still another topic is the whole question of the budget, which comes up so often in the actors' comments. Which productions were oppressed by budget pressure and which seemed to be affected very little? What did that pressure, or lack of it, do to make the productions differ?

The actors themselves, of course, spend most of their attention on the roles they performed, and it would be interesting to compare several actors of the same role, say of Caesar or Cassius or Mark Antony, and the ways different actors in various stages of acting careers in different kinds of production approach the same role or the art of acting in general. These are by no means the only possible topics for writing, and many will discover other topics of their own.

The main topic of study, of course, is the text of the play. That study will show that many problems, indeed, whole scenes from the text, are hardly mentioned in this book, but many others are discussed by the actors in some detail. A good essay can be built on discussing the various actors' reactions to the feeling that the character they are playing is marked by internal psychological contradictions. Another kind of problem that actors mention—a problem not always easy to see from reading the text of the play—is the ways used in a production to keep the audience interested, or mistakes that were made in keeping the attention of the audience.

Most ambitious of all might be to make a list of the most serious of these problems and then invent a "concept" for a possible production of the play that might solve or avoid as many of them as possible. Anyone who tries that will do well to remember that the audience for whom this play was originally written is, like its author, dead, and so any "concept" has to be calculated to appeal to the audience that might come to see it, a modern audience. Of course, the members of a modern audience, when they come to see Shakespeare, expect a production that suggests some flavor of the original production of Shakespeare's day, and they are right to do so. But they also expect, and they are right about this too, to see a play that is interesting and exciting and has something to say to them.

Index